How To Get 100% Employment or Zero Unemployment

How To Get 100% Employment or Zero Unemployment

Simon Abonia, MD

To order additional copies of this book, contact:
Xlibris Corporation
1-888-795-4274
www.Xlibris.com
Orders@Xlibris.com
98419

DEDICATION

To all my classmates, Teachers, Professors, Hospital Staff and offices employees who helped so well for so many years. To Rev. Padre Pedro Gomez professor of philosophy, mathematics and religion, who in 1953 appreciated and encourage me with *"The Youth Employment Savings Program", and with great wisdom and Intelligence,* in those years he helped with the Mayor and leaders of the town of Santander de Quilichao, Cauca, *prevent Violence or Terrorism in the region.*

Those who wrote letters in support of Health Insurance for a Lifetime: *Alex Cobo, MD, Universidad del Valle, 1957;* VicePresident Hoover Humphrey, The Director of Health and Human Services in NYC in 1968, Ms. Susanne A. Stoiber of The Department of Health, Education and Welfare in 1979; Senators Daniel Patrick Moynihan, Edward Kennedy, and the Department of Health of Ohio with Gov. George Voinovich in1993; VicePresident George H. Bush, Senators Alfonse D'Amato and Charles Schumer, and Commissioners of New York State Department of Health.

Letters from First Lady Hillary R. Clinton and President Bill Clinton; and with e-mails and letters from *Secretary Kathleen Sebelius* and President Barack Obama.

Meetings with George Wheatley, MD, MPH, FAAP, and Director of Suffolk County Department of Health, Marshal Lepidus, MD, Yellesphur Jayaram, MD.

Suffolk Pediatric Society: Michael Kaplan, MD, Bruce Platnik, MD, Albert Adler, MD; and a letter of approval for *The William Stewart Family Program or Housing Ownership.*

Working meetings with **Stuart** S. **Friedman,** MPS, Executive Director The **Suffolk County Medical Society**, and letters from Mr. **Mario V. Menghini**, Director, **MSSNY** Division of Socio-Medical Econmics.

With the Directors of Pediatrics Platon Collipp, MD, and Donald S. Gromisch, MD, at NCMC, and letters from *Mr.James A. Krauskopf, Commissioner of the New York City Human Resources Administration under Mayor Koch.*

Meeting with the AAP in 1994, and letters from David Annunziato, MD, Joseph L. Wright, MD, MPH, Joe M. Sanders, Jr, MD.

Letters from AMA **Executive Vice Presidents: James S. Todd, MD, Michael D. Maves, MD, MBA.**

Letters from the **AARP, Ms. Barbara Herzog, Director Health Care Campaign.** March 17, 1992

City Hall at Bolton Landing, letters from: Mr. Alexander Gabriels, former Town Supervisor, Mr. Dave Rosebrook, Assesor, **Peace Corps Volunteer, and the Staff at City Hall with** Mr. Ronald Conover, Town Supervisor.

Colombia: Letters from ANTONIO NAVARRO WOLFF, *Ministro de Salud and Alicia Victoria Arango Olmos, Chief of Staff of the Office of the President of Colombia, Alvaro Uribe Velez.*

"The Youth Employment Savings Program", with the help of Platon Collipp, MD, NCMC, letters from Senator Orrin G. Hatch 1981, Ms. Oprah Winfrey, **US Rep. Barbara Jordan, Dr. Adriano Mina, Michigan State University,** and University of Louisville, Kentucky.
"The longer young people are unemployed, the worse their future prospects become".—**8-17-11-NYTimes**

ACKNOWLEDGMENT

Thanks to my wife Cecilia R. Abonia and Children Juan Pablo Abonia and Samantha Wood Abonia, Victor Evrard and Claudia Marcella Abonia Evrard, my parents Hermelinda Abonia y Samuel Arrechea, Dna. Ana de Arrechea, *ALL my brothers and sisters,* my uncles/aunts: Dr. Eliecer Arrechea, Dna. Ema Sanchez de Arrechea, Sr. Pablo A. Zamora, Dna. Aurelia Arrechea de Zamora, Don. Rosendo Mezu, Dna. Maria Arrechea de Mezu, Don. Anibal Caicedo, Dna. Aura Rosa Arrechea de Caicedo, Don. Henry Alvaro Arrechea, Dna. Soila de Arrechea, Don. Rafael Ocoro, Dna. Guadalupe Abonia de Ocoro, Don. Manuel Abonia, Dna. Evangelina Banguero de Abonia, Don. Ernesto Abonia, Dna. Basilia de Abonia, Don Cupertino Lucumi Ulabarri, *Tia Josefina Abonia de Lucumi 99 years old,* <u>*Dr. Orlando Abonia Gonzalez y Dna. Maricel de Abonia,*</u> Don. Gaspar Balanta, Vilma Fany Orejuela de Balanta, Dr.*Gaspar Marino Balanta Orejuela,* Grand Parents Primitivo Arrechea y Leopoldina Arrechea; Simon Abonia y Hermelinda Mancilla Abonia whom died before I was born but whom I knew well for all that they did, starting with the wonderful house en la Quebrada, (Cauca), where I was born; *Dn. Francisco Castano, Dna. Raquel Savedra de Castano (Hotel Combeima), Don. Jose Dolores Martinez, Dna. Otilia Figueroa de Martinez,* Families, Relatives, Neighbors, Friends, workers and/or employees of the family, *who helped with their own philosophy of life and work.*

There is no Poverty but Unemployment, A Good Education or jobs stars before the child is born, all of them need F.E.M., which is A Good Education or Jobs.

INTRODUCTION

1-E—How to get 100% Employment or Zero Unemployment: with *A Good Education or jobs,* all students will be working before graduation, *and those who drop out will be working before they do, in any field they choose through the help of their teachers* and the Department of Education.

A Good *EDUCATION OR EMPLOYMENT ARE THE SAME THING;* A Good Education, Jobs or *F.E.M., in order to get 100% Employment or Zero Unemployment.* A Good *EDUCATION is a Job.*

In regard to **F.E.M.**, A Good Education or Jobs: (F = Family (Housing), work, *job* or profession for All . . . . E=Education for All, ... M=Medicine (Medical and Dental) or <u>Health Security For All And For a Lifetime, ...</u> In the United States, MEXICO and in Colombia a Good Education or jobs for All will decrease the crime rate more than **90%**; with <u>Health Security For All And For a Lifetime</u> this crime rate will decrease again more than 90%; and with *Family (HOUSING),* work, *job* or profession for *all* this crime rate will decrease again more than **90%**, reaching a reduction of the crime rate (**TERRORISM**) close to **99.9%** all over the country.

ALL Children (Students) *will have 10 years, 20 years and/or 25 to 30 years* of training/working *(A Good Education or Job)* at School, and close to *99% will find or create jobs* by themselves *before Graduation.*—*Bullies will not be tolerated <u>even for a second,</u> All children/students are working (STUDYING).*

A Good Education, Jobs or F.E.M.= JOBS (Like any other job, ALL Students, including Nurseries, Kindergarden, Primary Schools, ... Colleges, ... Universities, ... will earn a day work, an hour, a week, a month a year, ...). *No one will fail a year in the States; just like any other job.*—*Bullies will not be tolerated **even for a second**, All children/students are working (STUDYING).*

More than **95% will find or create jobs by themselves** and **less than 5% will need help from teachers** or the Department of Education.

A Good Education or *F.E.M. will add no extra cost to the Individual, Family or Government (Departments of: Housing, Education and Health); either in **United State**s, Mexico, **Colombia**, ...*

There is no Poverty but Unemployment, A Good Education or jobs stars before the child is born, all of them need **F.E.M., which is** A Good Education or Jobs.

2-M—**Individual Health Insurance** (Medical and Dental) **Paid at the Local Banks by Everyone and for a Lifetime, or** Long-term care insurance for ALL and *FOR A LIFETIME*.
Individual Health Insurance (Medical and Dental) **Paid at the Local Banks by Everyone and for a Lifetime and with** no **EXTRA** expenses to the Government, Family or Individual, *have all the benefits of the **Public Plan** including 100% **COMPETITION** or Universal Coverage for ALL citizens; and works very well with* the **President Obama's health reform** *of* **March 21, 2010.**

I) GOOD MEDICINE OR HEALTH INSURANCE (Paid by All) FOR A LIFETIME (DENTAL AND MEDICAL) IS THE KEY TO FIGHT *IGNORANCE OR POVERTY* **(Unemployment),** *GANGS,* **. . . II) WITH A HEALTHIER FAMILY (HOUSING), WORK, JOB, OR PROFESSION FOR** *ALL***; III) AND A GOOD EDUCATION OR JOBS (***100% Employment***) FOR** *ALL***, . . .** *(Pillars of Social Peace)*
F.E.M.= FAMILY (HOUSING), EDUCATION, MEDICINE.
Three Pillars of Social Peace.
"*We have Child Health Care-Crisis when one or more Children are Uninsured*".

There is no Poverty but Unemployment, A Good Education or jobs stars before the child is born, all of them need **F.E.M., which is** A Good Education or Jobs.

It is evident that: **"WITHOUT HEALTH INSURANCE FOR A LIFETIME THERE IS NO GOVERNMENT OR TRUE DEMOCRACY, BUT POVERTY** (Unemployment) **OR IGNORANCE, CRIME, VIOLENCE, . . . GANGS, TERRORISM, . . . IN THE POOR NEIGHBORHOODS, INNER CITIES, . . . DEVELOPING COUNTRIES** *and Illegal Immigration".*

<u>**3-F—Family Home**</u>**/Housing or Employment are The Same**. *With*"**FAMILY-MORTGAGE or SECURE-FAMILY-MORTGAGE"** the present <u>**Family Homes**</u> and the <u>New Family Homes or Mortgages</u> **<u>can be made Safe and Economically Sound by the Banks, the Government and the Business Community.</u>**

There is no Poverty but Unemployment, A Good Education or jobs stars before the child is born, all of them need **F.E.M., which is** A Good Education or Jobs.

A Good Education or **F.E.M.** is **The Social Security of ALL Children and the Youth** *(The Social Security of All Workers)*, that guarantees A Good Education for ALL; Work or Housing **(FAMILY-MORTGAGE or SECURE-FAMILY-MORTGAGE)** and <u>**Individual Health Insurance**</u> (Medical and Dental) <u>**Paid at the Local Banks by All and for a Lifetime,**</u> *and without Extra cost to the Government, Family or Individual;* <u>*making our Present Social Security economically safe and sound.*</u>

No Jobs? Young Graduates Make Their Own—December 13, 2010

Mr. Gerber, now twenty-seven, isn't a millionaire, but he's paid off his loans and doesn't have to live with his parents (he rents an apartment in Hoboken, New Jersey), and he thinks his experience can help other young people who face a daunting unemployment rate.

In October, Mr. Gerber started *the Young Entrepreneur Council to create a shift from a resume-driven society to one where people create their own jobs.* He says, "The jobs are going to come from the entrepreneurial level."(*New York Times*, December 13, 2010)

Editorial: Health Care and the Deficit

Congress can't fix the deficit *without a plan to rein in spending on health care.* Two bipartisan commissions have issued recommendations. (*New York Times*, December 13, 2010)

A Good Education or FEM: F= Family, Housing, Work, Jobs, or Profession for All = These Five Are the Same or Absolutely Necessary (Family, housing, work, jobs, or profession)

A good education, jobs, or FEM = *jobs* (like any other job, *all* students, including nurseries, kindergarten, primary schools, colleges, universities will earn a day work, an hour, a week, a month, a year). *No one will fail a year in Hawaii and in the rest of the States, just like any other job. Bullies will not be tolerated even for a second. All children/students are working (studying).*

How to Get 100 percent Employment or Zero Unemployment

A good education or FEM will add no extra cost to the individual, family, or government (Departments of Housing, Education, and Health) in either United States, Mexico, Colombia . . .

There is no poverty, but unemployment . . .

A Good Education for *All* Children is the fundamental part, which *is to triplicate the number of educators and duplicate the salary of all teachers and professors, forcing the department education budget to grow bigger every year, including the voluntarily* savings in *the Department of Education by all* citizens.

With the help of everyone, we will be able to *have long-term savings for all through the Department of education. It will* allow more than *three hundred million citizens* to save voluntarily and as much as possible at the Department of education in order to help finance a good education for all, *adding no extra cost to the government*, to the individual or to the family. Therefore, *raising (duplicating) the salary of all teachers and professors, and at the same time, triplicate the number of educators, forcing the Department of education budget to grow bigger every year.*

These *Long-term savings* in the Department of Education Is for the Payment of Educators Salary Only.

If we educate the children, we educate the entire family, and we educate the whole country . . .
See a good education or FEM = *jobs* (like any other job, *all* jobs, including nurseries, kindergarten, primary schools, colleges will earn a day work, an hour, a week, a month, a year.)

Charities, foundations, gifts, grants, or inheritance soon will start working or saving directly through the Department of education, and in the same way, those who win the lotto until they decide what they are going to do with it, in the meanwhile, will collect their interest (weekly, monthly . . .) if needed.

We at *Health for all* (November 03, 2009) and *For a Lifetime* are going to open a long-term savings account at the Department of education. With *more than three hundred million citizens doing the same, within the next few weeks or months, this savings will grow to one billion, two billion, or more, and will continue to grow,* forcing the government educational budget to grow bigger every year.

The Malpractice and Educational Insurance or Youth's Violence (Terrorism) and Crime Prevention with more than 60 percent of all premiums to go to the Department of education.

FEM is self-financed and emphasizes that *more than 90 percent of the real solution is the Department of Education* (it does triplicate the number of educators).

We have more than 2.2 million in prison, and here in the United States a good education for all will decrease the crime rate more than *90 percent,* with Health Security For All And For a Lifetime this crime rate will decrease again more than *90 percent,* and with family (*housing*), work, job, or profession for all, this crime rate will decrease again more than *90 percent,* reaching a reduction of the crime rate close to 99.9 *percent* all over the country. A Good *education* for *all* is the most important key (more than 90 percent of the real solution *is the Department of Education)* to end and to *prevent* crime, wars, or terrorism, and malaria in Colombia, *Mexico* and in many countries.

A good education or FEM is self-financed and emphasizes that more than 90 percent of the real solution is the Department of Education. (It does triplicate the number of educators.) With a good education or FEM, all students will be working before graduation.

Teaching candidates aplenty, but the jobs are few. (Winnie Hu)

In a profession long seen as recession proof, applications far outnumber the jobs available for educators. (New York)/*Region* (May 20, 2010)

The Port Washington district on Long Island is sorting through 3,620 applications for eight positions—the largest pool the superintendent has seen in his forty-one-year career.

In regard to a good education or FEM (F = Family (Housing) work for all, E = education for all, M = medicine (medical and dental), or

H = *Health Security for all and for a lifetime*) in the United States and in Colombia, a good education for all will decrease the crime rate more than 90 percent. With *health security for all and for a lifetime*, this crime rate will decrease again more than 90 percent, and with *family (housing), work, job, or profession for all*, this crime rate will decrease again more than 90 percent, reaching a reduction of the crime rate (*terrorism*) close to 99.9 *percent* all over the country—*A good education for all is the most important key (more than 90 percent of the real solution is with the Department of education) to end and to prevent crime, wars, or terrorism, and malaria in Colombia, South Africa, Peru, Mexico, Venezuela, and in many other countries.*

Family Home, Housing, or Employment
Is the Same

With family mortgage or *secure family mortgage*, the present *family homes* and the *new family homes* or mortgages *can be made safe and economically sound by the banks, the government, and the business community.*

A good education or FEM *is the social security for all children and youth (the social security of all workers)* that guarantees a good education for *all*. Work or housing (family mortgage or secure family mortgage) and *individual health insurance* (medical and dental) *paid at the local banks by all and for a lifetime and without extra cost to the government, family, or individual, will make our present social security economically safe and sound.*

With family mortgage or secure family mortgage, the present *family homes* and the new family homes or mortgages *can be made safe and economically sound by the banks, the government, and the business community.*

Sincerely,

Edgar S. Abonia, MD

In regard to a good education or FEM (F = family (housing) work for all, E = a good education for all, M = medicine (medical and dental) or health security for all and for a lifetime in the United States and in Colombia will decrease the crime rate more than *90 percent*. With *health security for all and for a lifetime*, this crime rate will decrease again more than 90 percent. With *family (housing), work, job, or profession for all,* this crime rate will decrease again more than *90 percent*, reaching a reduction of the crime rate (terrorism) close to *99.9 percent* all over the country. *A good education for all is the most important key (more than 90 percent of the real solution is with the Department of Education) to end and to prevent crime, wars, or terrorism, and malaria in Colombia, and in many other countries.*

(A) US nears Rescue Plan for Fannie, Freddie (August 15, 2008)

The government has prepared a plan to take control of troubled mortgage giants Fannie Mae and Freddie Mac, officials told the two companies, according to three sources familiar with the conversations.

Mortgage giants were blind to bubble (August 15, 2008)

Candidates Assess Fannie—Freddie Rescue
Mortgage Giants Were Blind to Bubble (August 15, 2008)

(B) Housing Lenders Fear Bigger Wave of Loan Defaults (August 15, 2008) (Vikas Bajaj)

Homeowners with good credit are falling behind on their payments in growing numbers, just as the problems with sub prime mortgages are leveling off.

(C) Woes Afflicting Mortgage Giants Raise Loan Rates (August 15, 2008) (Vikas Bajaj)

The troubles at Fannie Mae and Freddie Mac could deal another blow to the housing market as higher interest rates make it harder to refinance existing debts.

(D) A Glut of One-Bedroom Apartments (August 15, 2008) (Christine Haughney)

The inventory of one-bedroom apartments in Manhattan grows, apparently because buyers, particularly first-timers can't get mortgages.

(E) A good education or FEM is the social security of *all* children and youth *(the Social Security of all workers)* that guarantees a good education for *all*. Work or housing (family mortgage or secure family mortgage) and *Individual Health Insurance* (Medical and Dental) *Paid at the Local Banks by All and for a Lifetime, and without Extra cost to the Government, Family or Individual; making our Present Social Security economically safe and sound.*

A Good Education is the best solution for our environment and the global *warming crisis, and at the same time, we will* reach a reduction of *the crime rate or terrorism* by *more than 90 percent* all over the country and through *FEM. or peace this crime rate or* terrorism *will* reach a further reduction *close to 99.9 percent* all over the country.

Family Home/Housing, or Employment is the Same

Note—A Good Education or *FEM (F = Family* (Housing), work, jobs, or profession for All—these five are the same or absolutely necessary. *Family, Housing, work, jobs or profession*—THESE *Long-Term savings* in the Department of Education *are for payment of educators salary only.*

No Jobs? Young Graduates Make Their Own (December 13, 2010)

Mr. Gerber, now 27, isn't a millionaire, but he's paid off his loans and doesn't have to live with his parents (he rents an apartment in Hoboken, New Jersey). And he thinks his experience can help other young people who face a daunting unemployment rate.

In October, Mr. Gerber started *the Young Entrepreneur Council to create a shift from a resume-driven society to one where people create their own jobs.* He says, the jobs are going to come from the entrepreneurial level. (*New York Times*, December 13, 2010)

Editorial—Health Care and the Deficit

Congress can't fix the deficit *without a plan to rein in spending on health care.* Two bipartisan commissions have issued recommendations. (*New York Times*, December 12, 2010)

How to get 100 percent Employment or Zero Unemployment.

A Good Education or *FEM will add no extra cost to the individual, family, or government (Departments of Housing, Education and Health) in either United States, Mexico, Colombia . . .*

There is no poverty but unemployment . . .

A Good *Education or Employment Is the Same Thing.*

With **A Good Education or** FEM *all students will be working before graduation.*

If we educate *the children, we* educate *the entire family, and we* educate *the whole country . . .*

See a good education or FEM = *jobs* (like any other job, *all* including nurseries, kindergarten, primary schools, colleges will earn a day work, an hour, a week, a month a year.)

See a Good *education or FEM = 100 percent employment/ good education or FEM and the teachers are tolerant/ troublemakers/bullies . . . zero trouble makers/bullies with a good education or FEM.*

Homeownership stays at lowest level in a decade
(AP—two hours forty-eight minutes ago)
Republicans encouraged sub prime lending to borrowers with weak credit and fought off regulation of the industry, *despite warnings that many of those loans* had predatory terms. (November 2, 2010)

GOP Panelists Dissent on Cause of Crisis
(Sewell Chan, 11:55 p.m. ET)
Republican members of a panel examining *the causes of the financial crisis are expected to blame housing policies. (New York Times*, December 14, 2010)
  Tea Party Pressures G.O.P. to Reject Tax—Cut Deal

FamilyHome/Housing,orEmployment is the Same.

November 2, 2010

President Barack Obama
The White House
Washington DC 20500

Dear President Obama and *staff*:

We greatly appreciate your help *with family mortgage or secure family mortgage.* The present *family homes and the new family homes or mortgages can be made safe and economically sound by the banks, the government, and the business community. (Please review letters and e-mails to Ms. Valerie Jarrett,* secretaries Shawn Donovan and Arne Duncan.)

Family Home/Housing or Employment is the Same.

With family mortgage or secure family mortgage the present *family homes* and the new family homes, or mortgages *can be made safe and economically sound by the banks, the government, and the business community.*

A good education or FEM is *the social security of all children and youth (the* social security of all workers) that guarantees a good education for *all.* Work or housing *(family mortgage or secure family mortgage)* and *individual health insurance* (medical and dental) *paid at the local banks by all and for a lifetime and without extra cost to the government, family, or individual, making our present* social security *economically safe and sound.*

With family mortgage or secure family mortgage the present *family homes* and the new family homes or mortgages *can be made safe and economically sound by the banks, the government, and the business community.*

Sincerely,

Edgar S. Abonia, MD

In regard to **a good education** or FEM (F = Family (Housing), work for all, E =a good education for all, M = medicine (medical and dental) or health security for all and for a lifetime in the United States and in Colombia will decrease the crime rate by more than *90 percent.* With health security for all and for a lifetime this crime rate will decrease again by more than *90 percent.* With family *(housing), work, job, or profession for all,* this crime rate will decrease again by more than *90 percent,* reaching a reduction of the crime rate *(terrorism)* close to *99.9 percent* all over the country.—*A Good education for all is the most important key (more than 90 percent of the real solution is with the Department of Education) to end and to prevent crime, wars or terrorism, and* malaria *in Colombia and in many other countries.*

(A) US nears rescue plan for Fannie, Freddie (August 15, 2008)

The government has prepared a plan to take control of troubled mortgage giants Fannie Mae and Freddie Mac officials told the two companies, according to three sources familiar with the conversations.

Mortgage Giants Were Blind to Bubble (August 15, 2008)

Candidates Assess Fannie–Freddie Rescue Mortgage Giants were blind to bubble (August 15, 2008)

(B) Housing Lenders Fear Bigger Wave of Loan Defaults—(August 15, 2008— *Vikas Bajaj*)
Homeowners with good credit are falling behind on their payments in growing numbers, just as the problems with subprime mortgages are leveling off.

(C) Woes Afflicting Mortgage Giants Raise Loan Rates
(August 15, 2008—Vikas Bajaj)
The troubles at Fannie Mae and Freddie Mac could deal another blow to the housing market as higher interest rates make it harder to refinance existing debts.

(D) A Glut of One–Bedroom Apartments (August 15, 2008—Christine Haughney)
The inventory of one-bedroom apartments in Manhattan grows, apparently because buyers, particularly first-timers can't get mortgages.

(E) A Good Education or FEM is *the social security of all children and youth (the social security of all workers)* that guarantees a good education for *all*. Work or housing *(Family-mortgage or secure family mortgage)* and *individual health insurance* (medical and dental) *paid at the local banks by all and for a lifetime and without extra cost to the government, family, or individual, making our present social security economically safe and sound.*

A Good Education is the best solution for our environment and the global warming crisis, and at the same time, we will reach a reduction of *the crime rate or terrorism by more than 90 percent* all over the country, and through *FEM or peace, this crime rate or terrorism will* reach a further reduction *close to 99.9 percent* all over the country.

Family Home / Housing or Employment is the Same

Op-Ed—Money Won't Buy You Health Insurance

The market for health insurance is broken *even for those who are able to pay for it. (New York Times,* February 20, 2011)

The private insurance premium is stabilized at the present level for the next five to ten years and probably will go lower every year due to 100 percent competition or universal coverage.

It is fundamental for peace in the United States of America, and internationally in Mexico, Haiti, Colombia, Israel, and Palestine, Iraq, . . . It cost ten times less in developing countries.

We repeat, it will lower the *Medicaid and welfare population* by more than *80 percent, and those who at any time have insufficient funds will go automatically into Medicaid* with all its laws and regulations.

Health Care Overhaul Taking Root in Divided Nation

The Green

"AUTHORIZED TO BUY FOOD STAMPS, AT HIS OR HER LOCAL BANK"
(The Check System organizes and localizes Medical and Social Services...)

The Green Check is a MEDICAL HOME for Everyone and for a Lifetime.

NEW YORK STATE DEPARTMENT OF HEALTH AND HUMAN SERVICES		3-8-00		
JAIME RIVERA				618
100 WICKS ROAD		medicaid # A D 1 5 6 8 9 P	(PATIENT'S SOCIAL SECURITY)	1-17
BRENTWOOD, N.Y. 11717				326

LTC or CNYSHI # | 055 | 88 | 5039 |

MANUEL RIOS, M.D. PEDIATRICS
NANCY SMITH, M.D. OB/GYN
ROBERT COHEN, M.D. FAMILY PRACTICE
JOHN GAREL, DENTIST
LUIS JONES, PODIATRIST
NCMC out patient clinic, HIP clinics, Hope Pharmacy.....Managed Care, HMO's, UNIONS......

provider

SOCIAL SECURITY

| 503 | 37 | 9844 |

(patient's name and address).

Check is a **MEDICAL HOME.**

PAY TO THE ORDER OF

Manuel Rios, M.D. ... $ 44.10

FORTY-FOUR DOLLARS AND TEN CENTS. DOLLARS

The Cheese Manhattan Bank, N.A.
47 Vanderbilt Motor Parkway
Commack, N.Y. 11725

CHASE

		PENDING, SUMMER OR FALL DATE	
	FAMILY IMMUNIZATION complete.-		
MEMO ANNA RIVERA B.D. 3-25-02	age in years 18	1	15	18	35	36	55	5√	over 65	10/12/99	
(Children or dependent)	(.... to use the age in years of the youngest child or adult, in each box or adult, in each box or group...)		2000 ?....	

patient's signature Manuel Rivera

0280" 0002" 870"500492" 0018

To be deposited within 10 days.

If the individual or family needs PRICE CONTROL CHECKS OR MEDICAID-MEDICARE, they just order or request their checks at their local banks (...$100 to $2500....deductible at income tax time); if they do not have bank accounts they will get them from Medicaid or local banks authorized by the Department of Health and Human Services, with a review every 5 years if necessary. (. . . savings no waste. . .)
"If we are going to control costs, we need a system in which the decision makers feel pressure to provide high quality care and control costs. A part of the solution, the World Bank report argues, is to decentralize delivery and force deliverers to compete on cost and health outcomes. 7-2-93

NOTE: 1) Several young Mothers are Illiterate." They don't know the A,B,C's... 2) A newborn has his/her medicaid card in the mail for a year... (...unopened family mail...) 3) Many Newborns and children under 1 year of age or older get their Medicaid card Not Eligible.... IN THE MAIL, NEEDS NEW APPLICATION...., and then wait, and wait, and wait,....THE SAME HAPPENS WITH: Insurance Companies, Managed Care, SCHIP.... (please review letter dated June 18, 1998 to Dr. Howard A. Pearson, AAP).

Barriers must fall to child health care access, coverage, vows Dr. Alpert

"I have not forgotten her answer. She said: 'Doctor Alpert, when every day of your life someone slaps you in the face, and suddenly you're offered an ice cream cone, you're not sure it's for real.'"
— DECEMBER -1998 AAP NEWS

MEDICAID and CHIP are TOO TINY (... applications, paper-work or ICE CREAM....). CHIP and Medicaid are TOO TINY, they need to be integrated with: Medicare-Medicaid, Private Health Insurance, HMO's, UNIONS HEALTH INSURANCE, and LONG TERM CARE HEALTH INSURANCE for ALL and for a LIFETIME by ALLOWING all patients to PAY at the Local Banks, through Medicaid-Medicare: (CHIP is Medicaid, a new Medicaid or a new kind of Medicaid and only for children who APPLY... paperwork or ICE CREAM...).

"Through the check system, and without paperwork, each family or individual will control cost, and by January 31 of every year, more than 99% of those who use "Price Control Checks", will have refunded to Medicare-Medicaid directly from their savings or bank account, the amount used in the past year, up to the $500.00 deductible (...$100 to $2500... or more according to their income tax), including Interest at market rate. Those who can not refund the deductible, will continue on Medicare-Medicaid, until they are able to do so, and their number will decrease yearly." **"MEDICAID-MEDICARE IS MANAGED CARE."**

HEALTH SECURITY FOR ALL, IN THE AMERICAS, IT PREVENTS OR CHANGES "CRIME, WARS, VIOLENCE OR GUERRILLA WARFARE."

IT IS THE RESPONSIBILITY OF ALL PHYSICIANS (EVERYONE: PHYSICIANS, DENTISTS, NURSES, PHARMACISTS, SOCIAL WORKERS, ADMINISTRATORS, PROFESSIONALS, WORKERS.....AND EACH PERSON IN PARTICULAR) TO MAKE SURE ALL PATIENTS (PEOPLE) ARE ALLOWED TO PAY THROUGH THE INCOME TAX STRUCTURE FOR HEALTH INSURANCE THAT CAN'T BE TAKEN AWAY (DENTAL AND MEDICAL) AND FOR A LIFE TIME'

Liability Reform

Malpractice insurance through Income Tax: 1% of the gross income of all health care providers, will allow older providers, to continue working and creating more jobs, more than 90% of the "Malpractice Educational Fund or Insurance" will go to the *General Education of All Youths.*

"The fact of the matter is the private market is absolutely incapable of solving the nation's long-term-care crisis."
— Gail Shearer of Consumer Union

Welcome and share ....20%....50 %....80 %..
Hospitalization bills...) with all kinds of competition, including Private Health Insurance, HMO's, HIP, UNIONS.....

THE CHECK SYSTEMS SAVES: AND EDUCATES PATIENTS TO HAVE ONE PHYSICIAN WITH FREEDOM OF CHOICE. . . there is no paperwork.

Authorized Provider

signature, _____

use stamp always

MANUEL RIOS, M.D. PEDIATRICS
78 WICKS ROAD
BRENTWOOD, NEW YORK 11717
FOR DEPOSIT ONLY AT CHASE MANHATTAN BANK
ACC. #5.03 ″ 00035

medicaid # 529305989

a MEDICAL HOME.

(Medicare or Medicaid)

"It also doesn't make sense to create a whole new bureaucracy when one already exists.

90071 examen r.o.,TBC		$ 39.00
9321 immun. dne test		1.90
L557 laborat. urban.		3.20
Total		$44.10

A Pledge to Halt Medicaid Denials — States cited for widespread problems
'I can't say whether these are significant willful failures or mistakes.' – Medicaid official Nancy-Ann DeParle

This system or Long Term Care Health insurance for ALL will be integrated or copied by the rest of the Americas, including Canada, and in the majority of these countries like: Mexico, Colombia, Haiti, Peru, El Salvador...it will cost 10 times less...$60.00 deductible per year and $500.00 for a lifetime of the tax payer, family, or individual, therefore fighting IGNORANCE or poverty, and helping stabilize the population and economy (STUPID) or CRIME, WARS, VIOLENCE OR GUERRILLA WARFARE. MEDICINE, THE BEST MEDICINE FOR US ALL." IN THE AMERICAS IT PREVENTS OR CHANGES "CRIME, WARS, VIOLENCE OR GUERRILLA WARFARE."

The empowerment of everyone with savings and cost control. will reduce the Health Care Budget 30% or more the first year, mostly by 3 mechanism: NO WASTE (there is no paper work), COMPETITION by private practice, hospitals and clinics, HMO's, HIP, UNIONS, ...with FREEDOM OF CHOICE AND WITH TOTAL EMPOWERMENT. At the same time the check system with the local bank, eliminates fraud and/or abuse, or at least reduces it to a documented minimum and audited by patients and providers. This Health Insurance is balanced daily, locally and nationally (computers); and with a general or national positive budget balance yearly (like a good commercial or savings Bank....) ....there is no paperwork....

LONG TERM CARE or catastrophic health insurance for a lifetime by itself will reduce the welfare population more than 80%; they will become regular taxpayers, because it will offer equitable medical and dental care to all and anywhere, including mental health care, without paper work or bankruptcy due to illness at any age...

Health Insurance May Be No Insurance at All

The unexpected expense of a major illness cannot reasonably be budgeted for:

Researchers around the country who interviewed families caring for seriously ill loved ones found that nearly a third spend most or all of their life savings. "We were quite struck by the magnitude of the findings."

NEWSDAY, WEDNESDAY, DECEMBER 21, 1994

With the AMERICAN ACADEMY OF PEDIATRICS, MSSNY, the AARP (Mrs. Barbara Herzog), we need your help Dr. Bhavani Srinivasan, Dr. Ruby Malva, Dr. Susan Aronso, Dr. Luis Z.Cooper, Dr. Donald S. Gromisch, Mr. Stuart S. Friedman, M.P.S. & Mr. Mario V. Menghini, former Director Socio-Medical Economics, because Medicaid or Public Health needs to be integrated with "LONG TERM CARE for all, including THE UNBORN OR PERSONAL AND CATASTROPHIC HEALTH INSURANCE (HOSPITALIZATIONS AND NURSING HOMES) THAT CAN'T BE TAKEN AWAY, AND FOR A LIFETIME (everyone needs to be ALLOWED TO PAY at the LOCAL BANKS, through Medicaid-Medicare for "LONG TERM CARE FOR ALL, including THE UNBORN OR PERSONAL AND CATASTROPHIC HEALTH INSURANCE FOR A LIFETIME"), otherwise it does hurt Government's and People's RE-SPONSIBILITIES. It does hurt people's health, AND SPECIALLY HURT CHILDREN'S HEALTH (Dental and Medical). IT IS OFFERED VOLUNTARILY TO THE PEOPLE.

A Growing U.S. Affliction: Worthless Health Policies
THE NEW YORK TIMES SATURDAY, JANUARY 4, 1997

$5000.00 for a lifetime, and $500.00 deductible PER YEAR...$100 to $2500 or more), TO BE PAID at the Local banks through MEDICARE-MEDICAID.

The Green Check is a MEDICAL HOME for Everyone and for a Lifetime.

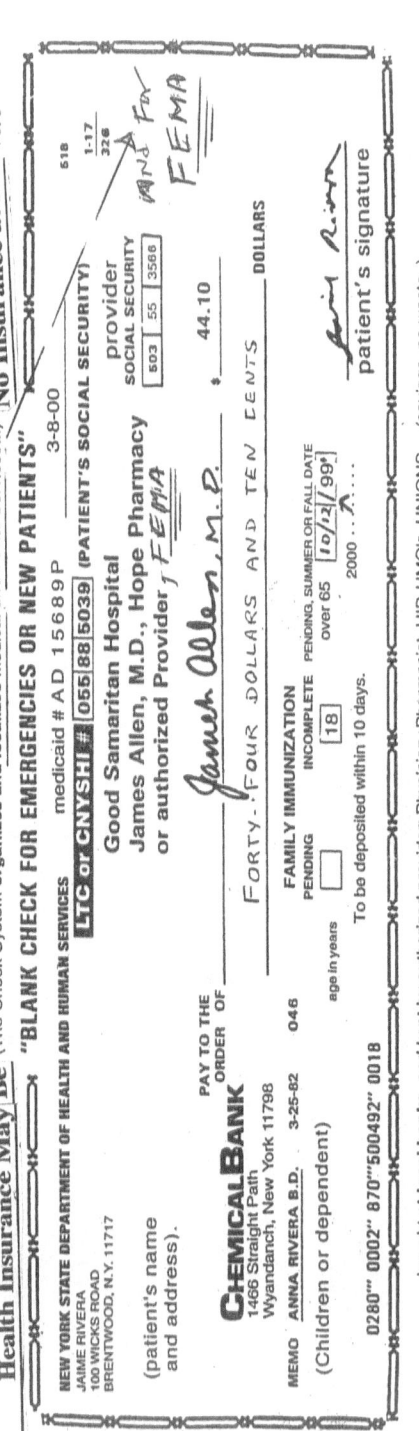

"BLANK CHECK FOR EMERGENCIES OR NEW PATIENTS"

NEW YORK STATE DEPARTMENT OF HEALTH AND HUMAN SERVICES   medicaid # AD 15689 P   3-8-00

LTC or CNYSH # 055 88 5039 (PATIENT'S SOCIAL SECURITY)

JAIME RIVERA
100 WICKS ROAD
BRENTWOOD, N.Y. 11717

PAY TO THE ORDER OF

(patient's name and address).

Good Samaritan Hospital
James Allen, M.D., Hope Pharmacy
or authorized Provider FEMA

provider
SOCIAL SECURITY
503 55 3566

James Allen, M.D. $ 44.10

CHEMICAL BANK
1466 Straight Path
Wyandanch, New York 11798

FORTY-FOUR DOLLARS AND TEN CENTS   DOLLARS

MEMO   ANNA RIVERA B.D.   3-25-82   046

(Children or dependent)

FAMILY IMMUNIZATION
PENDING   INCOMPLETE   PENDING, SUMMER OR FALL DATE
18   over 65   10/12/99
age in years   2000

To be deposited within 10 days.

patient's signature

0280 0002 870 500492 0018

518
1-17
226

... FEMA

... bought at local banks, and kept by authorized provider: Physician, Pharmacist, HIP, HMO's, UNIONS,.... (savings, no waste,.)

"*If we are going to control costs, we need a system in which the decision makers feel pressure to provide high quality care and control costs.* A part of the solution, the World Bank report argues, is to decentralize delivery and force deliverers to compete on cost and health outcomes. 7-2-93

"PRICE CONTROL, is our present system, it means NECESSARY SERVICES, and MEDICATIONS, with code #'s being used by Medicaid, Medicare and Insurance Companies."

"As Health Plan Comes Together Big Price Tag Comes Into Focus"   "Protection Called Inadequate or Too Expensive"

NOTE: 1) Several young Mothers are illiterate". They don't know the A,B,C's... 2) A newborn has his/her medicaid card in the mail for a year... (...unopened family mail...) 3) Many Newborns and children under 1 year of age or older get their Medicaid card Not Eligible.... IN THE MAIL, NEEDS NEW APPLICATION..., and then wait, and wait, and wait....THE SAME HAPPENS WITH: Insurance Companies, Managed Care, SCHIP,.... (please review letter dated June 18, 1998 to Dr. Howard A. Pearson, AAP).

Study: At-Risk Teens Shun MDs

"Uninsured adolescents were more likely to report forgone care than adolescents with continuous private or public insurance," the study added.   — NEWSDAY, WEDNESDAY, DECEMBER 18, 1999

MEDICAID and CHIP are TOO TINY (..., applications, paper-work or ICE CREAM....). CHIP and Medicaid are TOO TINY, they need to be integrated with: Medicare-Medicaid, Private Health Insurance, HMO's, UNIONS HEALTH INSURANCE, and LONG TERM CARE HEALTH INSURANCE for ALL, and for a LIFETIME by ALLOWING all patients to PAY at the Local Banks, through Medicaid-Medicare; (CHIP is Medicaid, a new Medicaid and only for children who APPLY....: paperwork or ICE CREAM....).

"Poverty Kills", or Ignorance. If everyone is ALLOWED TO PAY for good medicine or health insurance that can't be taken away, and for a lifetime, it will make the family and each individual, healthier and more self-sufficient. It will be offered to the people either voluntarily or mandatory by the U.S. Congress. IN THE AMERICAS, IT PREVENTS OR CHANGES "CRIME, WARS, VIOLENCE OR GUERRILLA WARFARE."

"Pay for Mental Health Care – and Save"

Authorized Provider

signature, _____ medicaid # 528305988

JAMES ALLEN, M.D. PEDIATRICS
79 WICKS ROAD
BRENTWOOD, NEW YORK 11717
FOR DEPOSIT ONLY AT CHASE MANHATTAN BANK
ACC. #5.03 ™ 08035388-

use stamp always →

"BLANK CHECK: need prior approval by:
Medicaid, Medicare, HMO's, UNIONS, or private insurance Co."
"To be deposited within 10 days."
Will take few more days to clear at bank.

Benefits everyone including the homeless, aids, and nursing homes claims

Children under **5 years of age** get many kinds of insurance, including Medicaid, **CHIP**, HMO's.... and in between they have **NOTHING** (no insurance), for weeks, months, or years; "The prescription; equal rate for all applicants - citizens (People): they need **LONG TERM CARE for ALL**, and for a **LIFETIME** (no paperwork, no applications for **ICE CREAM**).

Barriers must not fall to child health care access, coverage, vows Dr. Alpert: I have never forgotten her answer. She said: "Doctor Alpert, when every day of your life someone slaps you in the face, and suddenly you're offered an ice cream cone, you're not sure it's for real."

American Academy of Pediatrics
141 Northwest Point Blvd., Elk Grove Village, IL 60007-1098

October 8, 1998

Simon Abonia, MD
1618 New York Ave.
Huntington Station, NY 11746

Dear Dr. Abonia:

Thank you very much for the information you recently sent to me about your ideas regarding "Health Insurance for a Lifetime". The concept certainly seems consistent with the Academy's call for financial access to health care for all children, and so I will pass along some of your material to the AAP for inclusion in our discussions of that subject.
Perhaps we'll meet sometime to discuss your ideas further. Thanks very much for making me aware of your work.

Sincerely,

Joseph R. Zanga, MD, FAAP
President

CHIP is Medicaid, a new Medicaid or a new kind of Medicaid and only for children who APPLY.... paperwork or ICE CREAM.....

A Pledge to Halt Medicaid Denials
States cited for widespread problems
"I can't say whether these are significant willful failures or mistakes."
– Medicaid official Nancy-Anne DeParle

American Academy of Pediatrics
141 Northwest Point Blvd., Elk Grove Village, IL 60007-1098

February 10, 1999

Simon Abonia, MD
1618 New York, NY 11746

Dear Dr. Abonia:

There is much that you and I agree about regarding universal coverage. There are many mountains for us to climb before we reach this goal.
Certainly care for pregnant women (all women, of course) must be part of any comprehensive package.
Thank you for your efforts on behalf of universal coverage.

Sincerely,
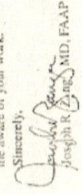
Joel J. Alpert, MD, FAAP
President

MEDICAID and CHIP are TOO TINY
(.... applications, paper-work or ICE CREAM....).

"MEDICAID-MEDICARE IS MANAGED CARE"

AIN'T NO MOUNTAIN HIGH ENOUGH.
DIANA ROSS AND THE SUPREMES"

Total $44.10

9321 Immun. the test 1.90
L657 laborat. urinan. 3.20
90071 examen r.o.TBC # 39.00

LONG TERM CARE
HEALTH INSURANCE
for ALL, including the
UNBORN AND FOR A
LIFETIME
OR
CATASTROPHIC NEW
YORK STATE HEALTH
INSURANCE FOR ALL
AND FOR A LIFETIME.
IT DOES COVER COSTS
OF MENTAL ILLNESS

For many years to come, Car Insurance and Workers Compensation must be left alone, as is it at the present time. and with their own paperwork.

THE CHECK SYSTEM ORGANIZES: PATIENTS AND PROVIDERS WITH SAVINGS OF 30% OR MORE.– IT HAS LOCAL BANK AND PUBLIC AUDIT, AND NO PAPERWORK.

LONG TERM CARE HEALTH INSURANCE for ALL, and FOR A LIFETIME, will ALLOW all patients to PAY (SHARE) for the ICE CREAM, through 100% COMPETITION, price control, savings or COST CONTROL by ALL; and without BARRIERS, not PAPERWORK....

One of the principal authors of the bill, *Democratic Senator Max Baucus of Montana says he laments not devoting more attention to cost control upfront as lawmakers worked to expand coverage.* "It gave detractors an opening," he said. (March 20, 2011)

Price control *is our present system; it means* necessary services *and* medications *with codes numbers being used by Medicare, Medicaid, HMO's, Insurance Companies . . . All will be able to use* the check system (Please review the three kind of checks *and the* money *chart by the Chase Manhattan Bank).*

Those on Medicare and without private health insurance will pay the premium within ten years through the income tax structure ($750 per year and for ten years), all will get the benefits of prescription drugs through the check system. We repeat those who have private health insurance will pay nothing.

March 29, 2010—Reviewed March 25, 2011

Individual Health Insurance (Medical And Dental) *Paid at the Local Banks by Everyone and for a Lifetime* or Long-Term Care Insurance for *All* and *for a Lifetime*

Individual health insurance (medical and dental) *paid at the local banks by everyone and for a lifetime and with* no *extra* expenses to the government, family, or individual *have all the benefits of the public plan, including 100 percent competition or universal coverage for* all *citizens and works very well with* the *President Obama's health reform of March 21, 2010.*

Senator Tom Harkin has made the correct diagnosis, and we have this lifetime solution or *individual health insurance* (medical and dental) *paid at the local banks by everyone and for a lifetime or* long-term care insurance for *all* and *for a lifetime, which* is a mandate for all through the income tax structure *and the biggest health insurance pool for all.*

The compliance always will be *100 percent* by just allowing people to pay for *individual health insurance for a lifetime* (long-term care insurance for all *and for a lifetime or individual health insurance* (medical and dental) *paid at the local banks by everyone and for a lifetime). (Those citizens who refuse to pay,* if they use the services, they will be billed through the income tax structure and they will continue with *individual health insurance for a lifetime and for all).*

We have this great opportunity to help immediately *after President Barack Obama signatures* (with a lot happiness and benefits to *all* patients) *the entire country, the Democrats, and the Republicans with* "the biggest health insurance pool for all," *which is a mandate for all through the income tax structure. Again Senator Tom Harkin has made the correct diagnosis—It's time to stop segregating people on the basis of their health. That's why insurance reform is so vital because the health insurance industry in this country is based on a flaw, and the flaw is the ratings are based on segregating people because of their health.*

This universal public plan for a lifetime is completely independent and always administered by Medicare Medicaid, and is *"the biggest health insurance pool for al,"* at the same time *fixes Medicare Medicaid.*

All hospitalization bills *(shared 20 percent/80 percent* with HMOs, private insurance, unions . . .) are paid *100 percent for all—*rich, *poor, or* homeless. *All bills are paid immediately and on the spot by all patients,* and *the daily expenses are paid by all through the income tax structure* or through HMOs, private insurance, unions, *health co-ops,* Medicaid-Medicare in the same way as it is now.

The private insurance premium is stabilized at the present level for the next five to ten years, and probably will go lower every year due to 100 percent competition *or universal coverage,* will lower the cost of health care *20 percent immediately* and for the *next five to ten years* (*universal coverage or 100 percent COMPETITION*). Those who already have any kind of health insurance *will pay nothing, and 20 percent* of the premium will be paid *by their own private insurance for three to ten years.* All hospitalization bills (shared *20 percent/80 percent* with HMOs, private insurance, unions) are paid *100 percent* for all *immediately and on the spot by all patients—rich,* poor or *homeless. It gives the government and the people the option of getting yearly subsidies* or to continue with *individual health insurance for a lifetime or* long-term care insurance for *all* and for *a lifetime with* the check system or cash, with complete accountability through the local banks; and solve a lot of political, economic and medical problems. It does work with any reform, system, or locality, and with *100 percent competition or coverage.*

It is fundamental for peace in the United States of America and internationally in Mexico, Haiti, Colombia, Israel, and Palestine, Iraq, and it cost ten times less in developing countries.

Please review previous *emails* with *the money chart by the Chase Manhattan Bank,* and special Check System *with the Green Check which is a Medical Home/or the Medical Home for everyone and for a lifetime.*

We repeat, it will lower the *Medicaid and welfare population* more than *80 percent, and* those *who at any time have insufficient funds will* go *automatically into Medicaid* with all its laws and regulations.

Price control *is our present system; it means* necessary services *and* medications, *with codes numbers being used by Medicare, Medicaid, HMO's, Insurance Companies; all will be able to use* the check system (Please review the three kinds of checks *and the* money *chart by the Chase Manhattan Bank).*

If one or more citizens are left without health insurance for a lifetime, we are not getting a good health care reform.—(Those citizens who refuse to pay and if they use the services, they will be billed through the income tax structure, and they will continue with individual health insurance for a lifetime and for all).—the biggest health insurance pool for all; at the same time we fix Medicare Medicaid.

"Small Ideas Won't Fix It." *Excellent health care reform now or individual health insurance for a lifetime and for all* covers 100 percent of uninsured people or more than 49 million for a lifetime, and with no extra expenses to the government, family, or individual.

Everyone who uses or need the check system through Medicaid Medicare has *$750* deductible per year *(for dental and medical services $100 to $3000 or more)*, any overpayment will be refunded each year through the income tax structure, at price control that at the beginning will be *80 percent of the customary local fees in each state.* When the medical profession and society in general lower once more the Medicaid and welfare population by 90 percent, the customary local fees in each state will be 90 percent, and so on. We can see that *100 percent of the customary fee* is nearly impossible when we consider the chronically ill and the handicapped. *The biggest health insurance pool for all* automatically lower the Medicaid and Welfare population 20 percent to 30 percent or more, even in our present time of *9.7 percent unemployment.*

Those on Medicare and without private health insurance will pay the premium within ten years through the income tax structure ($750 per year and for 10 years), and all will get the benefits of prescription drugs through the check system. We repeat those who have private health insurance will pay nothing.

Those who have insufficient funds will get their price control checks stamped Medicare Medicaid automatically by their own local banks, and their final balance will be calculated according to the income tax structure and Medicaid Medicare.

We repeat, it will lower the *Medicaid and welfare population* more than *80 percent, and those who at any time have insufficient funds will go automatically into Medicaid.*

With excellent health care reform now or *individual health insurance for a lifetime and for all,* the unemployment rate will be reduced to less than 9 percent within few weeks (probably *less than two months).* *All the people including* the uninsured will be referred to *their own local banks to pay* through the income tax structure for long-term care insurance for *all* and *for a lifetime* or *individual health insurance* (medical and dental) *Paid at the local banks by everyone and for a lifetime.*

Health Summit, 2010
House Speaker Nancy Pelosi Makes Opening Remarks at White House Health summit

So this bill is not only about the health security of America; it's about jobs. In its life it will create four million jobs, almost immediately, jobs again in the health care industry, but in the entrepreneurial world as well. Individual health insurance for a lifetime or long-term care insurance for *all* and *for a lifetime* is a mandate for all *through the income tax structure and* "the Biggest Health Insurance Pool for All. "

How to Control Soaring Health Care Costs
(Without this third player with Medicare Medicaid, there is no health security for a lifetime):

The medical savings account concept (cut your health insurance cost by 50 percent or more (mssny's *News Of New York,* January 1999) need to be offered to *100 percent* of the people. It works well with individual health insurance (medical and dental) paid at the local banks by all and for a lifetime, *without this third player with Medicare Medicaid, and there is no health security for a lifetime.*

Close to 100 percent of the uninsured *(more than 99 percent)* will open a medical savings account *on the advise of their own local banks,* where they will deposit at least the yearly deductible of about *$3000 ($100 to $3000 or more) according to the income tax structure and Medicaid Medicare.*

This *third player* is the best answer for our health care *problems; it has the* money, *solve all of them for a lifetime (individual health insurance* (medical and dental) *paid at the local banks by everyone and for a lifetime,* **or long-term care insurance for all and for a lifetime),** changing and improving our present health care system through *100 percent competition or universal coverage* because it is *administered by Medicare Medicaid and with 100 percent of the people through the* local banks, *doesn't need a New Agency and works very well with* the **President Obama's health reform** *of March 21, 2010.*

Sincerely,

Edgar S. Abonia, MD

Note–It gives the *government and the people* the option of getting *yearly subsidies* **or to continue with** *individual health insurance for a lifetime or* **long-term care insurance for *all*** and for *for a lifetime* with the check system *or cash, with complete accountability through the local banks,* and solve a lot of political, economic, and medical problems. It does work with any reform, system, *or locality,* and with *100 percent competition or coverage.*

This is a good summary of *individual health insurance for a lifetime and for all* that is completely independent and always administered by Medicare Medicaid:

Urging young Americans *(families and governments)* to anticipate old age and *for periods of no insurance, under employment or unemployment, homelessness, $7,500 for a lifetime (for hospitalization bills only), and $750 deductible* per year *($100 to $3000 or more)* to be paid *by* everyone, *family or individual at the local banks through Medicare Medicaid.* As you will see in the complete program—those who already have any kind of health insurance *will pay nothing (20 percent* of the premium will be paid *by their own private insurance for three to ten years),* and at the same time *those citizens who refuse or are unable to pay are covered 100 percent* and for a lifetime, until they are rehabilitated by the medical profession and society and able to continue paying *$250 per thirty years. (Those citizens who refuse to pay,* if they use the services, they will be billed through the income tax structure, and they will continue *with individual health insurance for a lifetime and for all).* "The Biggest Health Insurance Pool for All" at the same time we *fix Medicare Medicaid.*

Medicare Medicaid will ask Congress to increase the premium to $8000, $10,000, $15,000, or more when necessary. Individual health insurance (medical and dental) *paid at the local banks by everyone and for a lifetime* **or long-term care insurance for all and for a lifetime, and** at the same time we fix *Medicare Medicaid.*

Those on Medicare and without private health insurance will pay the premium within ten years through the income tax structure ($750 per year and for ten years), all will get the benefits of prescription drugs through the check system. *We repeat those who have private health insurance will pay nothing.*

The poor and the homeless will pay *$250* per year and for thirty *years*, and if they are unable to Pay Medicare Medicaid will take over until they are able to do so and/or rehabilitated by the medical profession and society.—*(100 percent competition or universal coverage).*

The dental health of all citizens will improve a great deal, specially adults without Medicaid nor health insurance, which is a real unemployment of *21 percent or more* without health insurance *(dental, we see it, look at it, and . . .)*

Note—(A) Our present health care system of private health insurance, HMOs, Unions, *health co-ops* will continue the same and will continue to improve through *100 percent competition or coverage,* and with the **President Obama's health reform** *of March 21, 2010.*

March 29, 2010

President Barack Obama
The White House
Washington, DC 20500

Dear President Obama and *Staff*:

We greatly appreciate your help with *individual health insurance* (medical and dental) *paid at the local banks by everyone and for a lifetime and with* no extra expenses to the government, family, or individual *have all the benefits of the public plan, including 100 percent competition or universal coverage for all citizens and works very well with* the *President Obama's health reform of March 21, 2010.*

Senator Tom Harkin has made the correct diagnosis, and we have this lifetime solution or individual health insurance (medical and dental) *paid at the local banks by everyone and for a lifetime or* long-term care insurance for *all* and for a lifetime *which is a mandate for all through the income tax structure and* "the biggest health insurance pool for all."

The compliance always will be *100 percent* by just allowing people to pay for *individual health insurance for a lifetime (long-term care insurance for all and for a lifetime or individual health insurance* (medical and dental) *paid at the local banks by everyone and for a lifetime).* (*Those citizens who refuse to pay, if they use the services, they will be billed through the income tax structure, and they will continue with *individual health insurance for a lifetime and for all).*

Please review previous e-mails with the *money* chart by the Chase Manhattan Bank, and special the check system *with the Green Check which is a medical home/or the medical home for everyone and for a lifetime.*

We repeat, it will lower the *Medicaid and welfare population* more than *80 percent, those who at any time have insufficient funds will go* automatically into Medicaid *with all its laws and regulations.*

Sincerely,
Edgar S. Abonia, MD

$7,500 for a lifetime (*for hospitalization bills only).* At the beginning, it will pay all hospitalization bills *under $10,500, all over the country,* sharing *20 percent/80 percent* with insurance companies, HMOs, unions, health co-ops . . .

"Urging young Americans (families) to anticipate old age" and for periods of *no* insurance, *under-employment, or unemployment, homelessness,*
The poor and the homeless will pay *$250* per year and for thirty *years*, if they are unable to pay Medicare Medicaid will take over until they are able to do so and/or rehabilitated by the medical profession and society.—(100 percent *competition* or universal coverage).

The Dental Health of all citizens will improve a great deal, specially adults without Medicaid nor health insurance, which is a real unemployment of *21 percent or more* without health insurance (Dental, *we see it, look at it, and . . .*).

April 25, 2010

From: msc@ama-assn.org <msc@ama-assn.org>
Subject: Medicare Medicaid Health Care System
To: healthforall03@yahoo.com
Date: Monday, March 30, 2009, 9:51 a.m.

Dear Dr. Abonia:

Thank you for sharing your thoughts on the role insurance plays in our health care system. Certainly our current structure is inadequate to meet the needs of many Americans, and we share your view that individuals should be empowered to take responsibility for their own insurance and for their own health care decisions.

Your material on individual health insurance for a lifetime and for all will be shared with the AMA policy staff.

Thank you again for writing. If you have any questions, please call AMA Member Relations at (800) 262-3211 or direct an e-mail to msc@ama-assn.org.

Sincerely,
American Medical Association

"You have clearly done some *hard thinking about how to assure universal access with as little bureaucracy as possible.* It has some real strengths." (AARP, Ms. Barbara Herzog, Director, Health Care Campaign. March 17, 1992)

"Small Ideas Won't Fix It." *Excellent health care reform now covers 100 percent of uninsured people or more than 49 million for a lifetime,* and with no *extra* expenses to the government, family, or individual *needs to be attached to* the *President Obama's health reform of March 21, 2010.*

Note—(A) Our present health care system of private health insurance, HMO's, Unions, *health co-ops* will continue the same and will continue to improve through *100 percent competition* and with **President Obama's health reform** *of March 21, 2010.*

"I do thank you for contacting me regarding your catastrophic health proposal. *Most interesting indeed."* (Hon. Senator Daniel P. Moynihan, December 11,1992).

The check system prevents *fraud and abuse close to 100 percent* because it *is audited daily by the local banks, patient, family or individual; all bills are paid immediately and on the spot by all patients; and needs to be attached to* the **President Obama's health reform** *of March 21, 2010.*

Money Won't Buy You Health Insurance

The market for health insurance is broken **even for those who are able to pay for it. (NY Times,** February 20, 2011)

The private insurance premium is stabilized at the present level for the next five to ten years and probably will go lower every year due to 100 percent competition or universal coverage. It is fundamental for peace in the United States of America, and internationally in Mexico, Haiti, Colombia, Israel and Palestine, Iraq, it cost ten times less in developing countries.

We repeat, it will lower the *Medicaid and welfare population* more than *80 percent, and those who at any time have insufficient funds will go automatically into Medicaid with all its laws and regulations.* Health care overhaul taking root in divided nation.

One of the principal authors of the bill, *Democratic Sen. Max Baucus of Montana, says he laments not devoting more attention to cost control up front as lawmakers worked to expand coverage.* "It gave detractors an opening," he said. (March 20, 2011)

Price control *is our present system; it means* necessary services *and* medications *with codes numbers being used by Medicare, Medicaid, HMO's, Insurance Companies. All will be able to use* the check system (Please review the three kind of checks *and the* money *chart by the Chase Manhattan Bank). Those on Medicare and without private health insurance will pay the premium within ten years through the income tax structure ($750 per year and for ten years), all will get the benefits of prescription drugs through the check system. We repeat those who have private health insurance will pay nothing.* (March 29, 2010—Reviewed March 25, 2011)

Individual health insurance (medical and dental) *paid at the local banks by everyone and for a lifetime or* long-term care insurance for *all* and *for a lifetime. Individual health insurance* (medical and dental) paid at the local banks by *everyone and for a lifetime and with* no extra expenses to the government, family, or individual *have all the benefits of the* public plan *including 100 percent* competition *or universal coverage for all citizens and works very well with* the *President Obama's health reform of March 21, 2010.*

Senator Tom Harkin has made the correct diagnosis, and we have this lifetime solution or individual health insurance (medical and dental) *paid at the local banks by everyone and for a lifetime or* long-term care insurance for all and for *a lifetime, which is a mandate for all through the income tax structure and* "The biggest health insurance pool for all."

The compliance always will be *100 percent* by just allowing people to pay for *individual health insurance for a lifetime (long-term care insurance for all and for a lifetime or individual health insurance* (medical and dental) *paid at the local banks by everyone and for a lifetime). (Those citizens who refuse to pay,* if they use the services, they will be billed through the income tax structure, and they will continue with *individual health insurance for a lifetime and for all).*

We have this great opportunity to help immediately *after President Barack Obama's signature* (with a lot happiness and benefits to all patients) *the entire country, the democrats and the republicans with "the Biggest Health Insurance Pool for All" which is a mandate for all through the income tax structure; again Senator Tom Harkin has made the correct diagnosis: It's time to stop segregating people on the basis of their health. That's why insurance reform is so vital because the health insurance industry in this country is based on a flaw. And the flaw is the ratings are based on segregating people because of their health.*

This universal public plan for a lifetime is completely independent and always administered by Medicare Medicaid, and is *"the Biggest Health Insurance Pool for All";* at the same time, fix Medicare Medicaid. All hospitalization bills *(shared 20 percent/80 percent* with HMOs, private insurance, unions) are paid *100 percent for all*—rich, *poor,* or homeless. *All bills are paid immediately and on the spot by all patients* and *the daily expenses are paid by all through the income tax structure* or through HMOs, private insurance, unions, *health co-ops,* Medicaid-Medicare, in the same way as it is now.

The private insurance premium is stabilized at the present level for the next five to ten years, and probably will go lower every year due to 100 percent competition *or universal coverage.* Will lower the cost of health care *20 percent immediately* and for the *next five to ten years (universal coverage or 100 percent competition);* those who already have any kind of health insurance *will pay nothing, 20 percent* of the premium will be paid *by their own private insurance for three to ten years.* All hospitalization bills shared *20 percent/80 percent* with HMOs, private insurance, unions) are paid *100 percent* for all *immediately and on the spot by all patients*—rich, poor, or *homeless. It gives the government and the people the option of getting yearly subsidies* or to continue with *individual health insurance for a lifetime or* long-term care insurance for *all* and for a lifetime *with* the check system or cash, *with complete accountability through the local banks and solve a lot of political, economic, and medical problems. It does work with any reform, system or locality, and with 100 percent* competition *or coverage. It is fundamental for peace in the United States of America and internationally in Mexico, Haiti, Colombia, Israel, and Palestine, Iraq, it cost ten times less in developing countries.* Please review previous e-mails with *the* money *chart by the Chase Manhattan Bank,* and special the check system *with the Green Check, which is a* Medical Home/ *or the Medical Home for everyone and for a lifetime.* We repeat, it will lower the *Medicaid and welfare population* more than 80 percent, and *those who at any time have insufficient funds will go automatically into Medicaid with all its laws and regulations.*

"Price control *is our present system, it means* necessary services *and medications with code numbers being used by Medicare, Medicaid, HMO's, insurance companies";* all *will be able to use* the check system. (Please review the three kind of checks *and the money chart by the Chase Manhattan Bank.)*

If one or more citizens are left without health insurance for a lifetime we are not getting a good health care reform.—(Those citizens who refuse to pay, if they use the services, they will be billed through the income tax structure, and they will continue with individual health insurance for a lifetime and for all).—"The Biggest Health Insurance Pool for All"; at the same time we *fix* Medicare Medicaid.

"Small Ideas Won't Fix It." *Excellent Health Care Reform Now or individual health insurance for a lifetime and for all, covers 100 percent of uninsured people or more than 49 million for a lifetime,* and with no extra expenses to the government, family, or individual. Everyone who uses or needs the check system through Medicaid Medicare has *$750* deductible per year *(for dental and medical services $100 to $3000 or more)*, and any overpayment will be refunded each year through the income tax structure at price control that at the beginning will be *80 percent of the customary local fees in each state.* When the medical profession and society in general lower once more the Medicaid and welfare population 90 percent, the customary local fees in each state will be 90 percent, and so on. We can see that *100 percent of the customary fee* is nearly impossible when we consider the chronically ill and the handicapped. *"The Biggest Health Insurance Pool for All"* automatically lower the Medicaid and welfare population 20 percent to 30 percent or more, even in our present time of *9.7 percent unemployment.*

Those on Medicare and without Private Health Insurance will pay the premium within ten years through the income tax structure ($750 per year and for ten years), all will get the benefits of prescription drugs through the check system. We repeat those who have private health insurance will pay nothing. Those who have insufficient funds will get their price-control-checks-stamped Medicare Medicaid automatically by their own local banks, and their final balance will be calculated according to the income tax structure and Medicaid Medicare.

We repeat, it will lower the *Medicaid and welfare population* more than *80 percent, and those who at any time have insufficient funds will go automatically into Medicaid.* With *excellent health care reform now or individual health insurance for a lifetime and for all,* the unemployment rate will be reduced to less than 9 percent within few weeks (probably *less than two months*), and *all* the people *including* the uninsured will be referred to *their own local banks to pay* through the income tax structure for long-term care insurance for all and for *a lifetime* or *individual health insurance* (medical and dental) *paid at the local banks by everyone and for a lifetime.*

Health Summit 2010
House Speaker Nancy Pelosi makes opening remarks at White House Health Summit

So this bill is not only about the health security of America; it's about jobs. In its Life, it will create four million jobs, 400,000 jobs almost immediately, jobs of, again, in the health care industry, but in the entrepreneurial world as well. Individual Health Insurance for a lifetime or long-term care insurance for all and for a lifetime *is a mandate for all through the income tax structure and "The Biggest Health Insurance Pool for All."*

How to control soaring health care costs (without this third player with Medicare Medicaid, there is no health security for a lifetime): The medical savings account concept (cut your health insurance cost by 50 percent or more, mssny's News Of New York, January 1999) need to be offered to *100 percent* of the people, and it works well with individual health insurance (medical and dental) paid at the local banks by all and for a lifetime, *without this Third Player with Medicare Medicaid, there is no health security for a lifetime.* Close to 100 percent of the uninsured *(more than 99 percent)* will open a medical savings account *on the advise of their own local banks,* where they will deposit at least the yearly deductible of about *$3000 (100 to $3000 or more) according to the income tax structure and Medicaid Medicare.*

This *Third Player* is the best answer for our Health Care *Problems, it has the money, solve all of then for a Lifetime (Individual Health Insurance* (Medical and Dental) *Paid at the local banks by everyone and for a lifetime or long-term care insurance for all and for a lifetime)* changing and improving our present Health Care System through *100 percent Competition or universal coverage*; because is *administered by Medicare Medicaid and with 100 percent of the People through the* Local Banks, *doesn't need a new agency and works very well with* the *President Obama's health reform of March 21, 2010.*

Sincerely,
Edgar S. Abonia, MD

Note—It gives the *government and the people* the option of getting *yearly subsidies* or to continue with *individual health insurance for a lifetime or* long-term care insurance for *all* and for a lifetiem *with* the check system *or cash, with complete accountability through the local banks;* and solve a lot of political, economics and medical problems. It does work with any Reform, System *or Locality,* and with *100 percent competition or coverage.*

This is a Good Summary of Individual Health Insurance for a *Lifetime and for All* that is completely independent and always administered by Medicare Medicaid:

"Urgingyoung Americans *(familiesandgovernments)* to anticipate old age" and *for periods of no insurance, under-employment or unemployment, homelessness, $7,500 for a lifetime (for hospitalization bills only),* and *$750 deductible per year (. . . $100 TO $3000 or more) to be paid by everyone, Family or Individual, at the Local Banks through Medicare-Medicaid.* As you will see in the complete program: those who already have any kind of Health Insurance *will pay nothing (20 percent* of the premium will be paid *by their own Private Insurance for three to ten years),* at the same time *those citizens who refuse or are unable to pay are covered 100 percent* and for a Lifetime, until they are rehabilitated by the Medical Profession and Society, and able to continue paying *$250 per thirty years.—(Those citizens who refuse to pay,* if they use the services, they will be bill through the Income Tax Structure, and they will continue *with Individual Health Insurance for a Lifetime and for All).—"The Biggest Health Insurance Pool for All";* at the same time we *FIX Medicare Medicaid.*

Medicare-Medicaid will Ask Congress to increase the premium to $8000, $10,000, $15,000, or more when necessary. (Individual Health Insurance (Medical and Dental) Paid at the Local Banks by Everyone and for a Lifetime or Long-term care insurance for all and *for a lifetime*); at the same time we FIX Medicare-Medicaid. *Those on Medicare and without Private Health Insurance will pay the premium within ten years through the Income-Tax Structure ($750 per year and for ten years), all will get the* *benefits of prescription drugs through The Check System. We repeat those who have Private Health Insurance will pay nothing.* The Poor and the Homeless will Pay *$250* per year and for thirty *years,* if they are

Unable to Pay Medicare-Medicaid will take over until they are able to do so and/or rehabilitated by the Medical Profession and Society.—*(100 percent competition or universal coverage). The Dental Health of all citizens* will improve a great deal, specially adults without Medicaid nor Health Insurance, which is a Real Unemployment of *21 percent or more* without Health Insurance *(Dental, we see it, look at it, and . . .).*

Note: (A) Our present Health Care System of Private Health Insurance, HMO's, Unions, *health co-ops, . .* will continue the same and will continue to improve through *100 percent competition or coverage,* and with the *President Obama's health reform of March 21, 2010.*

March 29, 2010
President Barack Obama
The White House
Washington, DC 20500

Dear President Obama and *staff:*

We greatly appreciate your help with Individual Health Insurance (Medical and Dental) Paid at the Local Banks by Everyone and for a Lifetime and with no Extra expenses to the Government, Family or Individual, *have all the benefits of the Public Plan including 100 percent competition or Universal Coverage for all citizens; and works very well with* the President Obama's health reform *of March 21, 2010.*

Senator Tom Harkin has made the correct diagnosis; and we have this lifetime Solution or Individual Health Insurance (medical and dental) *paid at the local banks by everyone and for a lifetime or long-term* care insurance for *all* and *for a lifetime*

which is a mandate for all through the income tax structure and "The Biggest Health Insurance Pool for All."

The compliance always will be *100 percent* by just allowing people to pay for *Individual Health Insurance for a Lifetime (Long-term care insurance for all and for a lifetime or Individual Health Insurance (Medical and*

Dental) Paid at the Local Banks by Everyone and for a Lifetime). *(Those citizens who refuse to pay,* if they use the services, they will be bill through the Income Tax Structure, and they will continue with *Individual Health Insurance for a lifetime and for all).*

Please review previous e-mails with *the money chart by the Chase Manhattan Bank,* and special the Check System *with the Green Check which is a medical home/or the medical home for everyone and for a lifetime.* We repeat, it will lower the *Medicaid and Welfare population* more than 80 percent, *those who at any time have insufficient funds will go automatically into Medicaid with all its laws and regulations.*

Sincerely,

Edgar S. Abonia, MD

$7,500 for a lifetime (for Hospitalization bills only) at the beginning it will pay all Hospitalization bills *under $10,500, all over the country,*

. . . Sharing *20 percent /80 percent* with Insurance Companies, HMOs, Unions, *health coops,*

"Urging young Americans *(families)* to anticipate old age" and for periods of *no* insurance, underemployment, or unemployment, homelessness. The poor and the homeless will pay $250 per year and for thirty *years,* if they are Unable to Pay Medicare-Medicaid will take over until they are able to do so and/or rehabilitated by the medical profession and society. *(100* percent *competition or universal coverage).*

The Dental Health of all citizens will improve a great deal, specially adults without Medicaid nor Health Insurance, which is a Real Unemployment of 21 percent or more without Health Insurance (Dental, . . . we see it, look at it, and . . .).

April 25, 2010

From: AMA
Subject: Medicare-Medicaid Health Care System
To: Abonia, MD
Date: Monday, March 30, 2009, 9:51 a.m.

Dear Dr. Abonia:

Thank you for sharing your thoughts on the role insurance plays in our health care system. Certainly our current structure is inadequate to meet the needs of many Americans, *and we share your view that individuals should be empowered to take responsibility for their own insurance and for their own health care decisions.*

Your material on *Individual Health Insurance for a Lifetime and For All* will be shared with the AMA policy staff.

Thank you again for writing. If you have any questions, please call AMA Member Relations at (800) 262-3211 or direct an e-mail to . . .

Sincerely,

American Medical Association "You have clearly done some *hard thinking about how to assure universal access with as little bureaucracy as possible.* It has some real strengths." AARP, Ms. Barbara Herzog, Director Health Care *Campaign.* March 17, 1992

"Small Ideas Won't Fix It." *Excellent Health Care Reform*

Now covers 100 percent *of uninsured people, or more than 49 million for a lifetime,* and with no extra expenses to the government, family or individual; *needs to be attached to* the President Obama's health reform of *March 21, 2010.*

Note: A) Our present Health Care System of Private Health Insurance, HMO's, Unions, health co-ops, will continue the same and will continue to improve through *100 percent competition* and with the *President Obama's health reform of March 21, 2010.*

"I do thank you for contacting me regarding your catastrophic health proposal. *Most interesting indeed." Hon. Senator Daniel P. Moynihan, 12-11-1992.* The Check System prevents *Fraud and Abuse close to 100 percent* because *is audited daily by the Local Banks, Patient, Family or Individual; all bills are paid immediately and on the spot by all patients; needs to be attached to the President Obama's health reform of March 21, 2010.* May 12, 2010

(These Long Term Savings are for payment of Educators Salary only). May 12, 2010

To Ms. Valerie Jarrett and Staff:

Please forward these e-mails to secretaries—Hilda L. Solis, Hillary Rodham Clinton, *Janet Napolitano, Ken Salazar, Robert Gates and Attorney General Eric H. Holder Jr.*

We don't have their e-mails. We at Health for all 03 and for a *lifetime,* each one is going to open a long-term savings account at the Department of Education and with *300 million citizens* doing the same, and *within the next few weeks or months this savings will grow to one billion, two billion, or more, and will continue to grow,* forcing the government educational budget to grow bigger every year. *(These long-term savings are for payment of educators salary only). To educate is to end and to prevent terrorism in the USA, Colombia, Mexico and in any other country or region.*

Foundations give boost to education
$506 million matching fund set up for federal grants
(*Donna Gordon Blankinship*)
(Updated 6:39 p.m. ET, Wednesday, April 28, 2010)

Seattle—A coalition of wealthy foundations is offering more than half a billion dollars to match federal grants meant to encourage educational reform, taking the pressure off schools scrambling to find the matching dollars they need to get the money.

Will the United States and Pakistan fight terrorism together? (May 5, 2010)

Abandoned water cooler causes Times Square scare (AP) (May 7 2010)

To Educate is to End and to Prevent Terrorism.

Teaching Candidates Aplenty, but the Jobs Are Few
(WINNIE HU)
In a profession long seen as recession-proof, applications far outnumber the jobs available for educators. (NY/REGION—MAY 20, 2010)

The Port Washington district on Long Island is sorting through 3,620 applications for eight positions—the largest pool the superintendent has seen in his forty-one-year career.

FEM is self-financed and emphasizes that more than 90 percent of the Real Solution is the Department of Education (It does Triplicate the number of Educators). With FEM all students will be working before graduation.

Teaching Candidates Aplenty, but the Jobs Are Few
(WINNIE HU)
In a profession long seen as recession-proof, applications far outnumber the jobs available for educators. (NY/REGION-MAY 20, 2010)

The Port Washington district on Long Island is sorting through 3,620 applications for eight positions—the largest pool the superintendent has seen in his forty-one-year career. In regard to F.E.M. (F= Family (Housing), work, . . . for All . . . E=Education for All, . . . M=Medicine (Medical and Dental) or Health Security For All And For a Lifetime, . . . In the United States and in Colombia a Good Education for All will decrease the crime rate more than *90 percent;* with Health Security For All And For a Lifetime this crime rate will decrease again more than *90 percent;* and with *Family (housing), work, job or profession for all* this crime rate will decrease again more than *90 percent,* reaching a reduction of the crime rate (*terrorism*) close to *99.9 percent* all over the country.—*A Good education for All is the most Important Key (more than 90 percent of the Real Solution is the Department of Education) To End and to prevent Crime, Wars or Terrorism, and Malaria in Colombia, South Africa, Peru, Mexico, Venezuela, . . . and in many other Countries.*

Teaching Candidates Aplenty, but the Jobs Are Few
(WINNIE HU)
In a profession long seen as recession-proof, applications far outnumber the jobs available for educators. (NY/REGION-MAY 20, 2010)

The Port Washington district on Long Island is sorting through 3,620 applications for eight positions — the largest pool the superintendent has seen in his forty-one-year career. FEM is self-financed and emphasizes that *more than 90 percent of the Real Solution is the Department of Education (It does Triplicate the number of Educators). With FEM all students will be working before graduation.*

Teaching Candidates Aplenty, but the Jobs Are Few
(WINNIE HU)
In a profession long seen as recession-proof, applications far outnumber the jobs available for educators. N.Y. / REGION-MAY 20, 2010—*The Port Washington districton Long Island is sorting through 3,620 applications for eight positions — the largestpool the superintendent has seen in his forty-one-year career.*

The Private Insurance premium is stabilized at the present level for the next five to ten years, and probably will go lower every year due to 100 percent COMPETITION or universal coverage.

A Good Education is the best Solution for our Environment and the Global warming Crisis, and at the same time we will reach a reduction of *the crime rate or TERRORISM more than 90 percent* all over the country; and through *FEM or Peace this crime rate or Terrorism will* reach a further reduction *close to 99.9 percent* all over the country. Through FEM. *in all corners of Mexico, the illegal immigration problem in the US-Mexican border will be reduced more than 90 percent.* (Sen. Joseph Biden: Blame immigration woes on Mexico).

FEM will add no extra cost to the individual, family, or government (Departments of Housing, Education and Health) in either United States, Mexico, or Colombia. The private insurance premium is stabilized at the present level for the next five to ten years, and probably will go lower every year due to 100 percent competition *or universal coverage. It is fundamental for peace in the United States of America and internationally in Mexico, Haiti, Colombia, Israel, and Palestine, Iraq . . . It cost ten times less in developing countries.*

We repeat, it will lower the *Medicaid and Welfare population* more than *80 percent, those who at any time have insufficient funds will go automatically into Medicaid with all its laws and regulations.* It gives the *Government and the people* the option of getting *yearly subsidies* or to continue with *individual health insurance for a lifetime or long-term* care insurance for *all* and *for a lifteime with* the Check System *or cash, with complete accountability through the local banks,* and solve a lot of political, economics, and medical problems. It does work with any reform, system *or locality,* and with 100 percent *competition* or coverage.

May 14, 2010

Dear *Ms. Valerie Jarrett, Secretaries: Kathleen Sebelius, Shaun Donovan,* Arne Duncan, Hilda L. Solis, Hillary Rodham Clinton, *Janet Napolitano, Robert Gates, Ken Salazar, Attorney General Eric H. Holder Jr.,* Mr. Ron Kirk, Mr. Aaron S. Williams, and Staff:

We greatly appreciate your help in order to recommend this program of FEM or *a good education for all, and with* no *extra* expenses to the government, family or individual to President Barack Obama. *At the same time, please review similar e-mails about Colombia that we will forward to you within few minutes.* We do need your help in order *to have long-term savings for all through the Department of Education—it will* allow all *300 million citizens* to save voluntarily and as much as possible at the Department of Education in order to help finance a good education for all, *adding no extra cost to the government* nor to the individual or family, therefore, *raising (duplicating) the salary of all teachers and professors,* and at the *same time triplicate the number of educators, forcing the department education budget to grow bigger every year.* Charities, foundations, gifts, grants, or inheritance will soon start working or saving directly through the Department of Education, and in the same way, those who win the lotto until they decide what they are going to do with it, in the meanwhile, they will collect their interest (*weekly, monthly*) if needed.

We at Health for all 03 and for a *lifetime*, each one is going to open a long-term savings account at the Department of Education and with *300 million citizens* doing the same, *within the next few weeks or months, this savings will grow to one billion, two billion, or more, and will continue to grow,* forcing the government educational budget to grow bigger every year. *(These long-Term savings are for payment of educators' salary only).*

The "malpractice and educational insurance or youth's violence (terrorism) and crime prevention," with more than 60 percent of all premiums to go to the Department of Education.

Teaching Candidates Aplenty, but the Jobs Are Few
(Winnie Hu)

In a profession long seen as recession proof, applications far outnumber the jobs available for educators. (NY/REGION—MAY 20, 2010)

The Port Washington district on Long Island is sorting through 3,620 applications for eight positions—the largest pool the superintendent has seen in his forty-one-year career.

FEM is self-financed and emphasizes that *more than 90 percent of the real solution is the Department of Education* **(it does triplicate the number of educators).**

Teaching Candidates Aplenty, but the Jobs Are Few
(Winnie Hu)
In a profession long seen as a recession proof one, applications far outnumber the jobs available for educators. (NY/REGION—MAY 20, 2010)

The Port Washington district on Long Island is sorting through 3,620 applications for eight positions—the largest pool the superintendent has seen in his forty-one-year career.

Through FEM *in all corners of Mexico, the illegal immigration problem in the US—Mexican border will be reduced more than 90 percent.*
(Sen. Joseph Biden: Blame immigration woes on Mexico)

FEM will add no extra cost to the individual, family, or government (Departments of Housing, Education, and Health) in either United States, Mexico, or Colombia.

Sincerely,
Edgar S. Abonia, MD

NOTE: These three programs *or FEM will add no extra cost to the Colombian and US governments.* They are programs *that exist at the present in the Colombia and to a major or a minor degree in all the countries on earth.* What we are doing is to cover *all Colombians, all people, all citizens, all children, without exception,* just adapting to the local political and economic realities. *"The economy, stupid. The people, stupid."*

FEM will add no extra cost to the individual, family, or government (Departments of Housing, Education, and Health). The end and prevention of terrorism in Colombia through the UN (France or the designated country) *also means the end and prevention of terrorism in Mexico and in many other countries.*

"Es un conflicto innecesario" (UN)
We repeat FEM is self-financed *and emphasizes that more than 90 percent of the Real Solution is with the Department of Education* (It does triplicate the number of Educators). With FEM all students will be working before graduation.

We need a *good education,* not the best possible education *but a G = For a Good Education—(All United States Citizens)*

Colombians, South Africans, Peruvians, and Mexicans need to be allowed to make long-term savings in the Department of Education (more than 90 percent of the real solution is with the Department of Education). The bigger the long-term savings, the bigger the investment in education by each one of these governments, including all the benefits of peace at home and abroad, and we will reach a reduction of *the crime rate (terrorism,* Police detains brother of Ohio teen shooter, one in ten schools are 'dropout factories' (AP), ... OR *A GOOD EDUCATION) close to 99.9 percent* all over the country.

We repeat *FEM is self-financed and emphasizes* that more than *90 percent* of the real solution is the Department of Education *(it does triplicate the number of educators).*

Teaching Candidates Aplenty, but the Jobs Are Few

(Winnie Hu)

In a profession long seen as recession proof, applications far outnumber the jobs available for educators.(NY/REGION, MAY 20, 2010)

The Port Washington district on Long Island is sorting through 3,620 applications for eight positions — the largest pool the superintendent has seen in his forty-one-year career.

FEM is self-financed and emphasizes that *more than 90 percent of the real solution is the Department of Education (It does triplicate the number of educators)*. With FEM, all students will be working before graduation.

Teaching Candidates Aplenty, but the Jobs Are Few

(Winnie Hu)

In a profession long seen as recession proof, applications far outnumber the jobs available for educators. N.Y./REGION, MAY 20, 2010

The Port Washington district on Long Island is sorting through 3,620 applications for eight positions—the largest pool the superintendent has seen in his forty-one-year career.

To Educate is to End and to Prevent Terrorism in the USA, Colombia, MEXICO and in any other country or region. (December 9, 2009)

Dear Senators: *Mary Landrieu, Blanche Lincoln, Maria Cantwell,* Frank R. Lautenberg, Mark Pryor, Tom Harkin, *Joe Lieberman, John Kerry and Staff:*

Please examine attachments with the Green Check which is a *medical home* /or The *medical home* for Everyone and for a lifetime and the chart (It has the *money*) supplied *by the Chase Manhattan Bank, NA.*

Close to 100 percent of the Uninsured (more than 99 percent) will open a medical savings account on the advise of their own local banks, where they will deposit at least the yearly deductible of about *$3000 ($100 TO $3000 or more)* according to the *income tax structure and Medicaid Medicare.*

The Check System can be used now in this Medicaid Medicare crisis and also with FEMA, and with individual and local banks accountability. "*price control* is our present system, it means *necessary services* and *medications*, with codes numbers being used by Medicare, Medicaid, HMOs, insurance companies"; *all will be able to use the Check System (please review the three kind of checks).*

Medicare Medicaid is managed care, *with the automatic help of the local banks computer system,* with 100 percent competition for all patients and providers, *and with all bills paid on the spot by the patient (the people), the cost control will become a reality.*

Again the patient always will be responsible for the payment of all bills, *immediately and on the spot; more than 99 percent of all hospitalization bills for hospitals and physicians will go through and less than 1 percent will be corrected mostly by HMO's, insurance companies, unions, Medicare Medicaid,* and a new check will be issued and send back to the patient (the people) for its signature. In the daily expenses will be less, probably less than 0.5 percent and will be corrected, and a new check will be issued and send back to the patient for his or her signature.

It has the strongest cost control and they are—100 percent competition for all patients and providers all over the country and for a lifetime, individual and local control, including the local banks, and the income tax structure, HMOs, private insurance, unions, The medical savings account concept *(notice that all these insurances will pay only 80 percent of all hospitalization bills on agreement with Medicare Medicare);* the patient (the people) always will be responsible for the payment of all bills, *immediately and on the spot.*

The Private Insurance premium has been *reduced 20 percent for the next three to ten years;* it is possible that after three to ten *years* the private insurance premium will continue the same or lower because 100 percent *competition* for *all* (patients and providers), *and with the New Congressional Approved Health Care Reform in 2009* those who already have any kind of health insurance will pay nothing *(20 percent of the premium will be paid by their own private insurance for three to ten years).* At the same time, those citizens who refuse or are unable to pay *are covered 100 percent and for a lifetime,* until they are rehabilitated by the medical profession and society, and able to continue *paying $250 per thirty years.* (Those citizens who refuse to pay, if they use the services, they will be billed through the income tax structure, *and they will continue with individual health insurance for a lifetime and for all).*

How to Control Soaring Health Care Costs

Give Employees Cash to Buy Care
Regina Herzlinger—

With the same budget that every American is using now for the health care of their family or individual, *we have solved the problem of the uninsured (all—rich, poor, homeless, young and old, children, and the entire family) for a lifetime and without paperwork or delay, and with no extra expenses to the government, family, or individual.*

The compliance always will be *100 percent* by just allowing people to pay for individual health insurance for a lifetime.

(Those citizens who refuse to pay, if they use the services, they will be billed through the income tax structure, *and they will continue with Individual Health Insurance for a Lifetime and for All*).

Obama's Health Care Speech to Congress

(Published September 9, 2009)
In the meantime, for those Americans, who can't get insurance today because they have pre-existing medical conditions, we will immediately offer low-cost coverage that will protect you against financial ruin if you become seriously ill. *This was a good idea when Senator John McCain proposed it in the campaign, it's a good idea now, and we should embrace it. Catastrophic health insurance or individual health insurance (medical and dental) paid at the local banks by everyone and for a lifetime and with no extra expenses to the government, family, or individual* needs to be included with the New Congressional Approved Health Care Reform in 2009,

Finally, many in this chamber—particularly on the Republican side of the aisle—have long insisted that reforming our medical malpractice laws can help bring down the cost of health care. I don't believe malpractice reform is a silver bullet, *but I have talked to enough doctors to know that defensive medicine may be contributing to unnecessary costs*. I know that the Bush administration considered authorizing demonstration projects in individual states to test these issues. It's a good idea, and I am directing my secretary of health and human services to move forward on this initiative today.

We believe that *this third player is one of the best answer for our Health Care Reform, it has the money*, solve all of then for a lifetime, changing and improving our present health care system through 100 percent competition; because it is *administered by Medicare Medicaid and* with 100 percent of the people through the local banks, doesn't need a new agency and need to be attached to the New Congressional Approved Health Care Reform In 2009.

Sincerely,

Edgar S. Abonia, MD

$7,500 for a lifetime (for **hospitalization bills only**). At the beginning, it will pay all hospitalization bills under $10,500, all over the country, *sharing 20 percent/80 percent* with insurance companies, HMOs, health co-ops, a public insurance if approved, and also a "trigger" or "fallback" public plan, if approved.

"Urging young Americans (families) to anticipate old age" *and for periods of no insurance, underemployment, or unemployment, homelessness.*

The poor and the homeless will pay *$250 per year and for thirty years,* if they are unable to pay Medicare Medicaid will take over until they are able to do so and/or rehabilitated through FEM—*(100 percent competition).*

Note—(A) Our present health care system of private health insurance, HMOs, health co-ops will continue the same and will continue to improve *through 100 percent competition, and with the New Congressional Approved Health Care Reform in 2009,* Medicare Medicaid will *ask Congress to increase the premium to $8000, $10,000, $15,000,* or more when necessary.

COUNTY OF SUFFOLK

PROMPT PAY
FAILED PROMISE

ROBERT J. GAFFNEY
SUFFOLK COUNTY EXECUTIVE

Lawsuits and legislation fail to ensure prompt payment from insurers. The AMA supports a federal prompt-pay law as the answer.

October 7, 1996

DEPARTMENT OF HEALTH SERVICES
MARY E. HIBBERD, M.D., M.P.H.
COMMISSIONER

Health Insurance *Paid by All and for a Lifetime* or

LONG TERM CARE HEALTH INSURANCE PAID BY ALL AND FOR A LIFETIME

With the Local Banks, there is **no paperwork** for a LIFETIME.

(children are sent back and for from CHIP (to Medicaid, and at the end nothing for many....)

Simon Abonia, M.D.
1618 New York Avenue
Huntington Station, New York 11746 (...for the *EMERGENCY ROOM crisis*

or high volume of *Uninsured patients,...*)

Dear Doctor Abonia:

Thank you for keeping me posted on "Low Cost Health Insurance Protection". I know it has taken a lot of your personal time, patience, and money for this project. However, it is not clear to me as to how anyone can provide full medical coverage for $5,000.00 in his/her lifetime. (it is only for payments of hospitalizations and nursing homes bills) (to help MEDICAID-MEDICARE,....).

Currently, I am not a Pediatric Medical Administrator in Hauppauge. I have been reassigned to Riverhead on a different assignment. Hence, I am forwarding the full package to Doctor Mary Hibberd, Commissioner, Department of Health Services, for her review. Any questions you may have may kindly be addressed to her office.

"Urging young Americans (*families*) to anticipate old age", and

insurance premium for every family or individual will be reduced proportionally ...20%....) and Private Health Insurance Companies, UNIONS, MANAGED unnity, Hospitals,...) for payments of hospitalization bills only.

oves Through Checks originated from *HOSPITALIZATION AND*

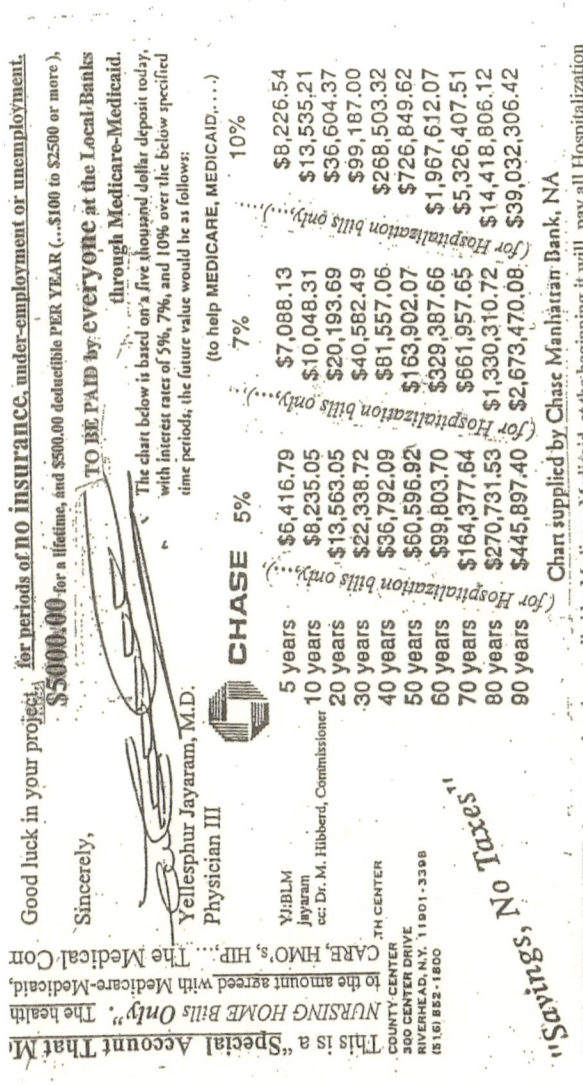

for periods of **no insurance**, under-employment or unemployment.
$5000.00 for a lifetime, and $500.00 deductible PER YEAR (...$100 to $2500 or more),

TO BE PAID by **everyone** at the Local Banks
through Medicare-Medicaid.

The chart below is based on a five thousand dollar deposit today,
with interest rates of 5%, 7%, and 10% over the below specified
time periods; the future value would be as follows:

(to help MEDICARE, MEDICAID,....)

CHASE	5%	7%	10%
	(for Hospitalization bills only.)	*(for Hospitalization bills only.)*	*(for Hospitalization bills only.)*
5 years	$6,416.79	$7,088.13	$8,226.54
10 years	$8,235.05	$10,048.31	$13,535.21
20 years	$13,563.05	$20,193.69	$36,604.37
30 years	$22,338.72	$40,582.49	$99,187.00
40 years	$36,792.09	$81,557.06	$268,503.32
50 years	$60,596.92	$163,902.07	$726,849.62
60 years	$99,803.70	$329,387.66	$1,967,612.07
70 years	$164,377.64	$661,957.65	$5,326,407.51
80 years	$270,731.53	$1,330,310.72	$14,418,806.12
90 years	$445,897.40	$2,673,470.08	$39,032,306.42

Chart supplied by Chase Manhattan Bank, NA

Good luck in your project,

Sincerely,

Yellesphur Jayaram, M.D.
Physician III

Yl:BLM
Jayaram
cc: Dr. M. Hibberd, Commissioner

COUNTY CENTER
300 CENTER DRIVE
RIVERHEAD, N.Y. 11901-3309
(516) 852-1800

This is a "Special Account That M...
to the amount agreed with Medicare-Medicaid,
CARE, HMO's, HIP,... The Medical Con...
NURSING HOME Bills Only". The health

"Savings, No Taxes"

Don't Be Fooled! Medicare Is a Huge Success

"Politically and Technically Complex, Medicare Defies a Sweeping Redesign", but
when we expand Medicare FOR A LIFETIME ($5000), from the UNBORN and the NEWBORN to the
ELDERLY, we fix Medicare, *without touching it*; and in the same way all *Public Hospitals and Clinics, MEDICARE
WILL PAY THE PREMIUM FOR ITS BENEFICIARIES IN 10 YEARS ($ 500 PER YEAR, it gives them the right to prescription
drugs.... with a deductible PER YEAR from...$100 to $2500,... or more according to their income-tax). IF THEY ARE UNABLE TO
PAY, MEDICAID-MEDICARE WILL TAKE OVER, UNTIL THEY ARE ABLE TO DO SO.*

A) This *THIRD PLAYER*, is managed and controlled by Medicare-Medicaid, at the beginning it will pay all Hospitalization
bills under $8000 all over the country. B) With Medicaid-Medicare, it will pay 20% of all Hospitalization bills of patients
from Private Health Insurance Companies, Unions, HMOs, HIP,... (they will pay the rest or 80%....of all Hospitalization bills.)

Health Insurance May Be (The Check System organizes and localizes Medical and Social Services...) No Insurance at All 4 of 5

"BLANK CHECK FOR EMERGENCIES OR NEW PATIENTS"

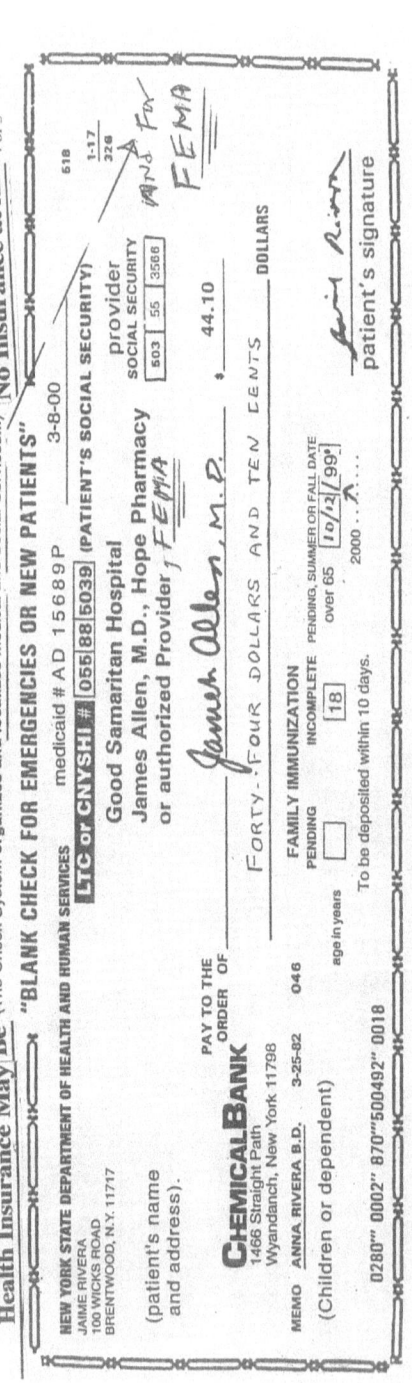

NEW YORK STATE DEPARTMENT OF HEALTH AND HUMAN SERVICES

LTC or CNYS-II # |055|88|5039| (PATIENT'S SOCIAL SECURITY)

medicaid # A D 1 5 6 8 9 P   3-8-00

JAIME RIVERA
100 WICKS ROAD
BRENTWOOD, N.Y. 11717

Good Samaritan Hospital
James Allen, M.D., Hope Pharmacy

(patient's name and address).

or authorized Provider ↑ FEMA

provider
SOCIAL SECURITY
|503 | 55 | 3566 |

PAY TO THE ORDER OF _____ James Allen, M.D.

CHEMICAL BANK
1466 Straight Path
Wyandanch, New York 11798

FORTY-FOUR DOLLARS AND TEN CENTS $ 44.10   DOLLARS

MEMO ANNA RIVERA B.D.   3-25-82   046

(Children or dependent)

FAMILY IMMUNIZATION

PENDING   INCOMPLETE   PENDING, SUMMER OR FALL DATE
          [18]   over 65 |10/12|/99'|

age in years

2000 ...?...

To be deposited within 10 days.

0280''' 0002'' 870'''500492'' 0018

patient's signature

... bought at local banks, and kept by authorized provider: Physician, Pharmacist, HIP, HMO's, UNIONS.... (savings, no waste..)

"If we are going to control costs, we need a system in which the decision makers feel pressure to provide high quality care and control costs. A part of the solution, the World Bank report argues, is to decentralize delivery and force deliverers to compete on cost and health outcomes. 7-2-93

"PRICE CONTROL is our present system, it means NECESSARY SERVICES, and MEDICATIONS, with code #'s being used by Medicaid, Medicare and Insurance Companies."

"As Health Plan Comes Together Big Price Tag Comes Into Focus"   *"Protection Called Inadequate or Too Expensive"*

NOTE: 1) Several young Mothers are **Illiterate**". They don't know the A,B,C's... 2) A newborn has his/her medicaid card in the mail for a year... (...unopened family mail...) 3) Many **Newborns** and children **under 1 year of age** or older get their Medicaid card **Not Eligible**.... IN THE MAIL, NEEDS NEW APPLICATION.... and then wait, and wait, and wait....THE SAME HAPPENS WITH: Insurance Companies, Managed Care, SCHIP.... (please review letter dated June 18, 1998 to Dr. Howard A. Pearson. AAP).

Study: At-Risk Teens Shun MDs
– NEWSDAY, WEDNESDAY, DECEMBER 18, 1999

"Uninsured adolescents were more likely to report forgone care than adolescents with continuous private or public insurance," the study added.

MEDICAID and CHIP are TOO TINY (..., applications, paper-work or ICE CREAM...). CHIP and Medicaid are TOO TINY, they
need to be integrated with: Medicare-Medicaid, Private Health Insurance, HMO's, UNIONS HEALTH INSURANCE, and LONG TERM CARE HEALTH INSURANCE for ALL and for a LIFETIME by ALLOWING all patients to PAY at the Local Banks, through Medicaid-Medicare: (CHIP is Medicaid, a new kind of Medicaid and only for children who APPLY.... paperwork or ICE CREAM....).

"Poverty Kills", or Ignorance. If everyone is ALLOWED TO PAY for good medicine or health insurance that can't be taken away; and for a lifetime, it will make the family and each individual, healthier and more self-sufficient. It will be offered to the people either voluntarily or mandatory by the U.S. Congress. IN THE AMERICAS, IT PREVENTS OR CHANGES "CRIME, WARS, VIOLENCE OR GUERRILLA WARFARE."

"Pay for Mental Health Care - and Save"

Authorized Provider

signature. _[signature]_ medicaid # 528305988

JAMES ALLEN, M.D., PEDIATRICS
78 WICKS ROAD
BRENTWOOD, NEW YORK 11717
FOR DEPOSIT ONLY AT CHASE MANHATTAN BANK
ACC. #5.03 ''' 0003536B-

use stamp always →

"BLANK CHECK: need prior approval by:
Medicaid, Medicare, HMO's, UNIONS, or private Insurance Co."
"To be deposited within 10 days."
Will take few more days to clear at bank.

Benefits everyone including the homeless, aids, and nursing homes claims

Children under **5 years of age** get many kinds of Insurance, including Medicaid, CHIP, HMO's....and in between they have **NOTHING** (no insurance), for weeks, months, or years; "The prescription: equal rate for all applicants.... citizens (People): they need **LONG TERM CARE for ALL and for a LIFETIME** (no paperwork, no applications or ICE CREAM).

Barriers must fall to child health care access, coverage, vows Dr. Alpert: I have never forgotten her answer, She said: "Doctor Alpert, when every day of your life someone slaps you in the face, and suddenly you're offered an ice cream cone, you're not sure it's for real."

American Academy of Pediatrics
141 Northwest Point Blvd., Elk Grove Village, IL 60007-1098

October 8, 1998

President Joseph R. Zanga, MD, Vice President Louis Z. Cooper, MD, Past President Robert E. Hannemann, MD, Executive Director Joe M. Sanders, Jr. MD

Board of Directors

Simon Abonia, MD
1618 New York Ave.
Huntington Station, NY 11746

Dear Dr. Abonia:

Thank you very much for the information you recently sent to me about your ideas regarding "Health Insurance for a Lifetime." The concept certainly seems consistent with the Academy's call for financial access to health care for all children, and so I will pass along some of your material to the AAP for inclusion in our discussions of that subject.

Perhaps we'll meet sometime to discuss your ideas further. Thanks very much for making me aware of your work.

Sincerely,

[signature]

Joseph R. Zanga, MD, FAAP

(CHIP is Medicaid, a new Medicaid or a new kind of Medicaid and only for children who APPLY.... paperwork or ICE CREAM....)

A Pledge to Halt Medicaid Denials
States cited for widespread problems
"I can't say whether these are significant willful failures or mistakes."
– Medicaid official Nancy-Anne DeParle

Total $44.10

9007f examen r.o.TBC $ 39.00
9321 Immun. una test   1.90
L667 laborat. urinan.   3.20

LONG TERM CARE HEALTH INSURANCE for ALL, including the UNBORN AND FOR A LIFETIME

OR

CATASTROPHIC NEW YORK STATE HEALTH INSURANCE FOR ALL AND FOR A LIFETIME.

IT DOES COVER COSTS OF MENTAL ILLNESS

For many years to come, Car Insurance and Workers Compensation must be left alone, as it is at the present time, and with their own paperwork.

THE CHECK SYSTEM ORGANIZES: PATIENTS AND PROVIDERS WITH SAVINGS OF 30% OR MORE. — IT HAS LOCAL BANK AND PUBLIC AUDIT, AND NO PAPERWORK.

LONG TERM CARE HEALTH INSURANCE for ALL, and FOR A LIFETIME, will ALLOW all patients to PAY (SHARE) for the ICE CREAM, through 100% COMPETITION, price control, savings or COST CONTROL by ALL; and without BARRIERS, nor PAPERWORK....

American Academy of Pediatrics
141 Northwest Point Blvd., Elk Grove Village, IL 60007-1098

February 10, 1999

President Joel J. Alpert, MD, Vice President Donald E. Cook, MD, Executive Director Joe M. Sanders, Jr. MD

Board of Directors

Simon Abonia, MD
1618 New York Ave.
Huntington Station, NY 11746

Dear Dr. Abonia:

There is much that you and I agree about regarding universal coverage. There are many mountains for us to climb before we reach this goal.

Certainly care for pregnant women (all women, of course) must be part of any comprehensive package.

Thank you for your efforts on behalf of universal coverage.

Sincerely,

[signature]

Joel J. Alpert, MD, FAAP
President

MEDICAID and CHIP are TOO TINY
(.... applications, paper-work or ICE CREAM....).

"MEDICAID-MEDICARE IS MANAGED CARE"

AIN'T NO MOUNTAIN HIGH ENOUGH.
DIANA ROSS AND THE SUPREMES."

The Green Check is a MEDICAL HOME for Everyone and for a Lifetime.

"AUTHORIZED TO BUY FOOD STAMPS, AT HIS OR HER LOCAL BANK"
(The Check System organizes and localizes Medical and Social Services...)

NEW YORK STATE DEPARTMENT OF HEALTH AND HUMAN SERVICES
JAIME RIVERA
100 WICKS ROAD
BRENTWOOD, N.Y. 11717

medicaid # AD 15689 P   3-8-00

513
1-17
326

LTC or CNYSHI# 055 88 5039 (PATIENT'S SOCIAL SECURITY)

MANUEL RIOS, M.D. PEDIATRICS
NANCY SMITH, M.D. OB/GYN
ROBERT COHEN, M.D. FAMILY PRACTICE
JOHN GAREL, DENTIST
LUIS JONES, PODIATRIST
NCMC out patient clinic, HIP clinics, Hope Pharmacy.....Managed Care, HMO's, UNIONS,.....

provider
SOCIAL SECURITY
503 37 9844

(patient's name and address).

Check is a MEDICAL HOME

PAY TO THE ORDER OF ___Manuel Rios, M.D.___   44.10

FORTY-FOUR DOLLARS AND TEN CENTS. . . . . DOLLARS

The Chase Manhattan Bank, N.A.
42 Vanderbilt Motor Parkway
Commack, N.Y. 11725

CHASE

MEMO ANNA RIVERA B.D. 3-25-82
(Children or dependent)

FAMILY IMMUNIZATION complete..
age in years 18 1 15 18 35 36 65 54
(.... to use the age in years of the youngest child or adult, in each box or group...)

PENDING, SUMMER OR FALL DATE
over 65 10/12/99
2000 ?....

patient's signature

To be deposited within 10 days.

0280 0002 870 500492 0018

If the individual or family needs PRICE CONTROL CHECKS OR MEDICAID-MEDICARE, they just order or request their checks at their local banks (...$100 to $2500,...deductible at income tax time); if they do not have bank accounts they will get them from Medicaid or local banks authorized by the Department of Health and Human Services, with a review every 5 years if necessary. (. . . savings no waste . . .)

"If we are going to control costs, we need a system in which the decision makers feel pressure to provide high quality care and control costs. A part of the solution, the World Bank report argues, is to decentralize delivery and force deliverers to compete on cost and health outcomes. 7-2-93

NOTE: 1) Several young Mothers are illiterate". They don't know the A,B,C's... 2) A newborn has his/her medicaid card in the mail for a year... (...unopened family mail...) 3) Many Newborns and children under 1 year of age or older get their Medicaid card Not Eligible.... IN THE MAIL, NEEDS NEW APPLICATION.... and then wait, and wait, and wait,...THE SAME HAPPENS WITH: Insurance Companies, Managed Care, SCHIP,... (please review letter dated June 18, 1998 to Dr. Howard A. Pearson, AAP).

Barriers must fall to child health care access, coverage, vows Dr. Alpert

"I have never forgotten her answer. She said: 'Doctor Alpert, when every day of your life someone slaps you in the face, and suddenly you're offered an ice cream cone, you're not sure it's for real.'"

– DECEMBER - 1998 AAP NEWS

MEDICAID and CHIP are TOO TINY (.... applications, paper-work or ICE CREAM,...). **CHIP** and Medicaid are **TOO TINY**, they need to be integrated with: Medicare-Medicaid, **Private Health Insurance, HMO's, UNIONS HEALTH INSURANCE,** and **LONG TERM CARE HEALTH INSURANCE for ALL** and for a **LIFETIME** by **ALLOWING** all patients to **PAY** at the **Local Banks,** through Medicaid-Medicare; (*CHIP is Medicaid, a new Medicaid or a new Medicaid and only for children who APPLY.... paperwork or ICE CREAM,...).* "Through the check system, and without paperwork, each family or individual will control cost, **and by January 31 of every year,** more than 99% of those who use "Price Control Checks" will have refunded to Medicare-Medicaid directly from their savings or bank account, the amount used in the past year, up to the $500.00 deductible (...$100 to $2500... or more according to their income tax), **including interest at market rate.** Those who can not refund the deductible, will continue on Medicare-Medicaid, until they are able to do so, and their number will decrease yearly." **"MEDICAID-MEDICARE IS MANAGED CARE."** "MEDICAID-MEDICARE IS MANAGED CARE." HEALTH SECURITY FOR ALL, IN THE AMERICAS, IT PREVENTS OR CHANGES "CRIME, WARS, VIOLENCE OR GUERRILLA WARFARE."

IT IS THE RESPONSIBILITY OF ALL PHYSICIANS (EVERYONE: PHYSICIANS, DENTISTS, NURSES, PHARMACISTS, SOCIAL WORKERS, ADMINISTRATORS, PROFESSIONALS, WORKERS,... AND EACH PERSON IN PARTICULAR) TO MAKE SURE ALL PATIENTS (PEOPLE) ARE ALLOWED TO PAY THROUGH THE INCOME TAX STRUCTURE FOR HEALTH INSURANCE THAT CAN'T BE TAKEN AWAY (DENTAL AND MEDICAL), AND FOR A LIFETIME".

Welcome and share (...20%...50%...80%...
Hospitalization bills...) with all kinds of
competition, including Private Health Insurance,
HMO's, HIP, UNIONS,....
Authorized Provider

signature, _____

use stamp always ➤

THE CHECK SYSTEMS SAVES; AND
EDUCATES PATIENTS TO HAVE
ONE PHYSICIAN WITH FREEDOM OF
CHOICE... there is no paperwork.

medicaid # 529305009

a MEDICAL HOME.

MANUEL RIOS, M.D. PEDIATRICS
78 WICKS ROAD
BRENTWOOD, NEW YORK 11717
FOR DEPOSIT ONLY AT CHASE MANHATTAN BANK
ACC. #5.03" 00035

(Medicare or Medicaid)

"It also doesn't make sense to create a whole new bureaucracy when one already exists.

9007† examen r.o.TBC $ 39.00
9321 immun. the test 1.90
L557 laborat. urinan 3.20
_____
Total $44.10

Liability Reform
Malpractice insurance through
income tax: 1% of the gross income
of all health care providers, will allow
older providers, to continue working
and creating more jobs, more than
90% of the Malpractice Educational
Fund or Insurance will go to the
General Education of All Youths."

"The fact of the matter
is the private market is
absolutely incapable of
solving the nation's
long-term-care crisis."
— Gail Shearer of
Consumer Union

A Pledge to Halt Medicaid Denials – States cited for widespread problems

"I can't say whether these are significant willful failures or mistakes. – Medicaid official Nancy-Ann DeParle

This system or Long Term Care Health Insurance for ALL will be integrated or copied by the rest of the Americas, including Canada, and in the majority of these countries like: Mexico, Colombia, Haiti, Peru, El Salvador...It will cost 10 times less...$50.00 deductible per year and $500.00 for a lifetime of the tax payer, family, or individual, therefore fighting IGNORANCE or poverty, and helping stabilize the population and economy (STUPID) of each of these countries. "PREVENTIVE MEDICINE, THE BEST MEDICINE FOR US ALL." *IN THE AMERICAS IT PREVENTS OR CHANGES "CRIME, WARS, VIOLENCE OR GUERRILLA WARFARE."*

The empowerment of everyone with savings and cost control, will reduce the Health Care Budget 30% or more the first year, mostly by 3 mechanism: NO WASTE (there is no paper work), COMPETITION by private practice, hospitals and clinics, HMO's, HIP, UNIONS, ...with FREEDOM OF CHOICE AND WITH TOTAL EMPOWERMENT. At the same time the check system with the local bank, eliminates fraud and/or abuse, or at least reduces it to a documented minimum and audited by patients and providers. This Health Insurance is balanced daily, locally and nationally (computers); and with a general or national positive budget balance yearly (like a good commercial or savings Bank...) ....there is no paperwork....

LONG TERM CARE or catastrophic health insurance for a lifetime by itself will reduce the welfare population more than 80%; they will become regular taxpayers, because it will offer equitable medical and dental care to all and anywhere, including mental health care, without paper work or bankruptcy due to illness at any age....

A Growing U.S. Affliction: Worthless Health Policies

THE NEW YORK TIMES SATURDAY, JANUARY 4, 1992

Health Insurance May Be No Insurance at All

The unexpected expense of a major illness cannot reasonably be budgeted for:

Researchers around the country who interviewed families caring for seriously ill loved ones found that nearly a third spend most or all of their life savings. "We were quite struck by the magnitude of the findings."

NEWSDAY, WEDNESDAY, DECEMBER 21, 1994

With the **AMERICAN ACADEMY OF PEDIATRICS**, MSSNY, the AARP (Mrs.Barbara Herzog), we need your help **Dr. Bhavani Srinivasan, Dr. Ruby Malva, Dr. Susan Aronso, Dr. Luis Z.Cooper,** Dr. Donald S. Gromisch, Mr. Stuart S. Friedman, M.P.S. & Mr. Mario V. Menghini, former Director Socio-Medical Economics, because *Medicaid or Public Health needs to be integrated with* "LONG TERM CARE for all, including THE UNBORN OR PERSONAL AND CATASTROPHIC HEALTH INSURANCE (HOSPITALIZATIONS AND NURSING HOMES) THAT CAN'T BE TAKEN AWAY, AND FOR A LIFETIME (everyone needs to be ALLOWED TO PAY at the LOCAL BANKS, through *Medicaid-Medicare* for "LONG TERM CARE FOR ALL, including THE UNBORN OR PERSONAL AND CATASTROPHIC HEALTH INSURANCE FOR A LIFETIME"), otherwise it does hurt Government's and People's RE-SPONSIBILITIES. It does hurt people's health, AND SPECIALLY HURT CHILDREN'S HEALTH (Dental and Medical). *IT IS OFFERED VOLUNTARILY TO THE PEOPLE.*

THE WHITE HOUSE
WASHINGTON

January 16, 1996

Edgar Simon Abonia, M.D.
46 Wagon Wheel lane
Huntington Station, NY 11746

Dear Dr. Abonia:

Thank you for writing to share your health
care proposals. My staff and I appreciate
your taking time to convey your thoughts to
us, and we will keep your ideas in mind as
discussions on the federal budget continue.

Sincerely,

Jennifer Klein
Senior Policy Analyst

$5000.00 for a lifetime, and $500.00
deductible PER YEAR(...$100 to $2500 or
more), TO BE PAID at the Local Banks
through MEDICARE-MEDICAID.

The Green Check is a MEDICAL HOME for Everyone and for a Lifetime.

February 28, 2009 and June 5, 2010

An Updated or Practicing Professional Peace Corps Volunteers through the UN, Working with F.E.M. and for ALL citizens, is the best answer to Prevent and Stop War, Terrorism or Crime.

We need **"The Internationally Peace Corps Volunteers through the UN, Working with F.E.M. and for ALL citizens",** where each Country will permit its Professionals (carpenters, shoe makers and repair, plumbers, physicians, dentist, engineers, Teachers, FARMERS, ...) to go, and they will go on their own budget or expenses for at least two years; they will sign and agreement with "**The Internationally Peace Corps Volunteers through the UN"** that when they comeback they will get this NORMAL salary that has been accumulated, this salary is guarantee for ALL Countries by **"The Internationally Peace Corps Volunteers through the UN ", Working with F.E.M. and for ALL citizens.**

Note: if they work only one month, or more, they will be compensated for those months in the same way.

We believe that **5%, 10%, . . . or 20%** will stay permanent as citizens, they also will get their FULL accumulated salary if they made less than **50%** of their agreed regular Salary, if they made more than **50%, ... 90%, . . . they will get only 50%** of their agreed regular Salary; we can see that there is no **EXTRA** expenses to the Government, Family or Individual, <u>and is less expensive than one **_uninjured soldier_**</u>.

Each country has their own military commands and with the UN military commands and armies they will give the **OK** for **"The Internationally Peace Corps Volunteers through the UN, Working with F.E.M. and for ALL**

citizens", to start working or practicing their professions.

The great majority of the **The Internationally Peace Corps Volunteers through the UN**, more than **90%** *always will come from the neighboring countries* which is the Real UN, (. . . . more than **60%** will come from the same country or IMMIGRATION/brain drain in reverse).

We have Peace in Northern Ireland, next will be Colombia, Israel and Palestine, ...Iraq, ...

The UN are: France or the designated country, and the neighboring and brotherly countries of *Panama, Venezuela, Brazil, Peru, Ecuador y Bolivia (some Caribbean countries and* **MEXICO** *will be included).—-F.E.M. is Peace and with the UN, IT CAN BE DONE.*

For example in Colombia we only need Peace through the UN most probably *(With F.E.M. or PEACE more than 80% of ALL Colombians will be working Full Time Immediately, and less than 10% will need direct help or F.E.M., and without Extra cost to the Government, Family or Individual)*; but Haiti need right away 5,000 to 10,000 *(or more because the earthquake of January 12, 2010) of The* **Internationally Peace Corps Volunteers**: 8,000 will come from the US, 1000 from Canada, 1000 from the rest of Americas including MEXICO, *and some from other countries;* more than **60%** will be citizens of Haiti. The same way for North and South Korea, Israel and Palestine, Iraq, . . .).

In each and every country **"The Internationally Peace Corps Volunteers through the UN, Working with F.E.M. and for ALL citizens"**, they just go and practice their profession, either Private or with the Local Government.

F.E.M. is action for ALL: (E=Education (A Good Education or jobs) for All, . . . **M=Medicine** (Medical and Dental) or <u>Health Security For All And For a Lifetime,</u> . . . *F= Family (HOUSING), work, job or profession for ALL).*

NOTE: because the earthquake of January 12, 2010 Haiti probably will need more than **90,000** of **The Internationally Peace**

Corps Volunteers: about **40,000** will come from the US (more than **60%** will be citizens of Haiti), **10,000** from Canada, MEXICO, and the rest of Americas, and about 30,000 from the other countries of the world (more than **60%** will be citizens of Haiti). The same way for North and South Korea, Israel and Palestine, Iraq, ...).

Better care now in Haiti, but how long?
Four months after devastating quake, the country's impoverished are getting the best health care of their lives. NYTimes-5-12-10.—-**Individual Health Insurance** (Medical and Dental) **Paid at the Local Banks by Everyone and for a Lifetime.**

It is Fundamental for Peace in the United States of America, **and internationally in Mexico, Haiti, Colombia, Israel and Palestine, Iraq, ... it cost 10 times less in developing countries.**

Better care now in Haiti, but how long?
Four months after devastating quake, the country's impoverished are getting the best health care of their lives. NYTimes-5-12-10.—-**Individual Health Insurance** (Medical and Dental) **Paid at the Local Banks by Everyone and for a Lifetime.**

Sincerely,

Edgar S. Abonia, MD

$7,500.00 for a lifetime *(for Hospitalization bills only)* at the beginning it will pay all Hospitalization bills **under $10,500.00, all over the country,** . . . . Sharing **20%/80%** with Insurance Companies, HMOs, *health co-ops,* . . . .

"Urging young Americans *(families)* to anticipate old age" and for periods of **no** insurance, **under-employment or unemployment, homelessness,** . . . .

NOTE: A) Our present Health Care System of Private Health Insurance, HMO's, Unions, **health co-ops,** . . . . will continue the same and will continue to improve through **100% COMPETITION** *or coverage,* and with the **President Obama's health reform** *of March 21, 2010.*

The Poor and the Homeless will Pay **$250** per year and for **30 years**, if they are Unable to Pay Medicare-Medicaid will take over until they are able to do so and/or rehabilitated by the Medical Profession and Society.—*(100% COMPETITION or universal coverage).*

The Dental Health of all citizens will improve a great deal, specially adults without Medicaid nor Health Insurance, which is a Real Unemployment of **21% or more** without Health Insurance **(Dental,** . . . . **we see it, look at it, and** . . . .**).**

It gives the **Government and the people** *the option of getting* *yearly subsidies* or to continue with *Individual Health Insurance for a Lifetime or* Long-term care insurance for ALL and *FOR A LIFETIME with* The Check System or CASH, **with complete accountability through the Local Banks;** and solve a lot of political, economics and medical problems. *It does work with any Reform,*

*System **or Locality**, and with 100% COMPETITION or coverage.*

*It is Fundamental for Peace in the United States of America, **and internationally in Mexico, Haiti, Colombia, Israel and Palestine, Iraq**, ... <u>it cost 10 times less in developing countries</u>.*

Teaching Candidates Aplenty, but the Jobs Are Few
By WINNIE HU

In a profession long seen as recession-proof, applications far outnumber the jobs available for educators. N.Y. / REGION-MAY 20, 2010—*The Port Washington district on Long Island is sorting through 3,620 applications for eight positions — the largest pool the superintendent has seen in his 41-year career.*

F.E.M. is self-financed and emphasizes that *more than 90% of the Real Solution is the Department of Education* (It does Triplicate the number of Educators).—With F.E.M. ALL STUDENTS WILL BE WORKING BEFORE GRADUATION.

Teaching Candidates Aplenty, but the Jobs Are Few
By WINNIE HU

In a profession long seen as recession-proof, applications far outnumber the jobs available for educators. N.Y. / REGION-MAY 20, 2010—*The Port Washington district on Long Island is sorting through 3,620 applications for eight positions — the largest pool the superintendent has seen in his 41-year career.*

NOTE: **F.E.M.: F= Family** (Housing), work, jobs or profession for All===these Five are the same or absolutely necessary: **Family, Housing, work, jobs or profession**, ... —-THESE *Long Term* **SAVINGS** IN THE Department of Education ARE FOR PAYMENT OF *Educators* <u>SALARY ONLY.</u>

These three programs or F.E.M. *will add no Extra cost to the US and Colombia governments*, they are programs that exist at the present in the US, *and to a mayor or minor degree in ALL the countries on earth,* what we are doing is to cover ALL Americans, <u>ALL</u> People, ALL Citizens, ALL Children, without exception, just adapting to the local political and economic realities. **"The economy, stupid", "The people, stupid".**

F.E.M. will add no extra cost to the Individual, Family or Government (Departments of: Housing, Education and Health). *The End and Prevention of Terrorism in Colombia through the UN (France or the Designated Country) also means The End and Prevention of Terrorism in MEXICO and in many other countries.*

"Es un conflicto innecesario" . . ." UN.

THIS IS F.E.M. and we need it . . . :

Presidente electo de E.U. designa equipo para ayudar a la clase media afectada por crisis económica

Estará dirigido por el vicepresidente electo, **Joe Biden, e incluye a los secretarios de Salud, Educación y Trabajo.** Su labor arrancará el próximo 20 de enero, cuando inicia la nueva administración.

1 comentario.

Through F.E.M. *in All corners of Mexico, the* **Illegal Immigration Problem** *in the US-Mexican border will be reduced more than **90%.**—(Sen. Joseph Biden: Blame immigration woes on Mexico).** F.E.M. will add no extra cost to the Individual, Family or Government (Departments of: Housing, Education and Health); either in **United State**s, Mexico, **Colombia, Brazil,** Venezuela, **France**, Spain, **Switzerland,** . . . .*

F.E.M. is PEACE in many Places or Countries and with the UN (France or the Designated Country), IT CAN BE DONE.

We have Peace in Northern Ireland, next will be Colombia, Israel and Palestine, ...Iraq, ...

The UN are: France or the designated country, and the neighboring and brotherly countries of **Panama, Venezuela, Brazil, Peru, Ecuador y Bolivia** *(some Caribbean countries and* **MEXICO** *will be included).—F.E.M. is Peace and with the UN, IT CAN BE DONE.*

The UN can not tolerate "Machine gun Leaders, **Terrorists or Unemployed people of 100%",** of any Kind or Place; and in the same way Countries or Governments can not tolerate "Machine gun Leaders, **Terrorists or Unemployed people of 100%**", of any Kind or Place.

F.E.M. is Peace and with the **UN (France);** we at **HEALTHFORALL03,** we are ready to start working as soon as possible. *With the Volunteers we are going to be working in one Colombian City or location for Three, Six or Twelve months until the Job is done All over Colombia*; helping, with **ALL COLOMBIANS** to **end Misery or poverty,** *and without Extra cost to the Government, Family or Individual.*—Esto es posible asi como "La Cumbre de Río, más que lo esperado"; . . . y en menos de **24 horas**
▪ ▪ ▪ ▪

Teaching Candidates Aplenty, but the Jobs Are Few
By WINNIE HU
In a profession long seen as recession-proof, applications far outnumber the jobs available for educators. N.Y. / REGION-MAY 20, 2010—*The Port Washington district on Long Island is sorting through 3,620 applications for eight positions—the largest pool the superintendent has seen in his 41-year career.*

F.E.M. is self-financed and emphasizes that *more than 90% of the Real Solution is the Department of Education* **(It does Triplicate the number of Educators).**—With F.E.M. ALL STUDENTS WILL BE WORKING BEFORE GRADUATION.

Teaching Candidates Aplenty, but the Jobs Are Few
By WINNIE HU

In a profession long seen as recession-proof, applications far outnumber the jobs available for educators. N.Y. / REGION-MAY 20, 2010—*The Port Washington district on Long Island is sorting through 3,620 applications for eight positions — the largest pool the superintendent has seen in his 41-year career.*

To Educate with Jobs, *is to End and to Prevent Terrorism in the USA, Colombia, MEXICO and in any other country or region.*

Will the U.S. and Pakistan fight terrorism together?—5-4-10

Foundations give boost to education

$506 million matching fund set up for federal grants

By DONNA GORDON BLANKINSHIP

updated 6:39 p.m. ET, Wed., April 28, 2010
SEATTLE—A coalition of wealthy foundations is offering more than half a billion dollars to match federal grants meant to encourage

education reform, taking the pressure off schools scrambling to find the matching dollars they need to get the money.

Will the U.S. and Pakistan fight terrorism together?—5-4-10

Abandoned water cooler causes Times Square scare (AP)—5-7-10

To Educate with Jobs, is to End and to Prevent Terrorism.

REFERENCES (TOTAL= 14):

1—Who Cooked the Planet?

By PAUL KRUGMAN

Published: July 25, 2010 *NYTIMES*

2—Foundations give boost to education

$506 million matching fund set up for federal grants
By DONNA GORDON BLANKINSHIP updated 6:39 p.m. ET, Wed., April 28, 2010

3—As Health Costs Soar, G.O.P. and Insurers Differ on Cause

By ROBERT PEAR, March 4, 2011 NYTimes

4—Op-Ed: Money Won't Buy You Health Insurance

The market for health insurance is broken, *even for those who are able to pay for it.* *NYTime*-February 20, 2011

5—Mortgage giants were blind to bubble (August 15, 2008)

Candidates Assess Fannie–Freddie Rescue
Mortgage Giants Were Blind to Bubble (August 15, 2008)

(B) Housing Lenders Fear Bigger Wave of Loan Defaults (August 15, 2008) (Vikas Bajaj)
Homeowners with good credit are falling behind on their payments in growing numbers, just as the problems with sub prime mortgages are leveling off.

(C) Woes Afflicting Mortgage Giants Raise Loan Rates (August 15, 2008) (Vikas Bajaj)
The troubles at Fannie Mae and Freddie Mac could deal another blow to the housing market as higher interest rates make it harder to refinance existing debts.

(D) A Glut of One-Bedroom Apartments (August 15, 2008) (Christine Haughney)
The inventory of one-bedroom apartments in Manhattan grows, apparently because buyers, particularly first-timers can't get mortgages.

6—London Riots Put Spotlight on Troubled, Unemployed Youths in Britain

By LANDON THOMAS Jr. and RAVI SOMAIYA
Published: August 9, 2011 *NYTIMES*

7—Meten en cintura a la saluddelosmáspobres—*Napoleón*

Franco—**El Tiempo,** Viernes 13 de noviembre de 1998

8—Bolivia: <u>Un niño desnuda al sistema de salud boliviano</u>

Por <u>Grover Cardozo</u> [2010-04-09]

9-It's Still the Economy, Stupid

How would President Clinton get 14 million Americans back to work? See his 14 ideas in this week's Newsweek cover story. **Read more**.—6-24-11

10—"It Takes More Than Schools to Close Achievement Gap" The New York Times on August 9, 2006. **F.E.M. or A Good EDUCATION for All is the most Important Key (more than 90% of the Real Solution** *is the Department of Education)* **To End and to PREVENT Crime, Wars or Terrorism, and MALARIA in Colombia, MEXICO and in many Countries.**

11—*"Health Insurance May be no Insurance at All"*.

"The unexpected expense of a major illness cannot reasonably be budget for"

Researches around the country who interviewed families caring for seriously ill loved ones found that nearly a third spend most or all of their life savings. "We were quite struck by the magnitude of their findings," NEWSDAY December 24, 1994.

12—*Don't Be Fooled: Medicare Is a Huge Success*—*NYTimes 2000.*

13—*"Politically and Technically Complex, Medicare Defies a Sweeping Redesign"*—*NYTimes 2000; but when we expand Medicare for a Lifetime ($7500) from the Unborn and the Newborn to the Elderly, we fix Medicare, without touching it; and in the same way all Public Hospitals and Clinics.*—*Those on Medicare and without Private Health Insurance will pay the premium within 10 years through the Income-Tax Structure ($750 per year and for 10 years),* and with a deductible PER YEAR for the Daily Expenses of . . . $100 TO $3000 or more *through the Income-Tax Structure*; **all will get the benefits of prescription drugs through The Check System;** if they are Unable to Pay Medicare-Medicaid will take over until they are able to do so and/or rehabilitated by the Medical Profession and Society.—*(100% COMPETITION or universal coverage).We repeat those who have Private Health Insurance will pay nothing.*

14—A Growing U.S. Affliction: Worthless Health Policies—The New York Times, Saturday January 4, 1992.

The uninsured will be referred to the Local or Nearest Banks, <u>including the homeless and the very poor (. . . $165 per 30 years . . .) if they are unable to pay, Medicare-Medicaid will take over, until they are able to do so and/or rehabilitated through *F.E.M*,</u>*=Family (HOUSING), work, **job** or profession for **all; Good Education** for all, and **Good Medicine** for all (<u>Dental</u> and Medical), **three pillars of Social Peace;** <u>it is evident that these last Five are the same or absolutely necessary</u>:* Family, **Housing**, Work, **Job** or Profession.

www.ingramcontent.com/pod-product-compliance
Lightning Source LLC
Chambersburg PA
CBHW021237280526
45784CB00005B/2129